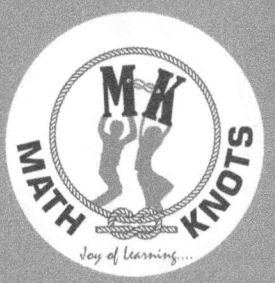

My Book

This book belongs to

Name: _____

Copy right © 2019 MATH-KNOTS LLC

All rights reserved, no part of this publication may be reproduced, stored in any system or transmitted in any form, or by any means, electronic, mechanical, photocopying, recording, or otherwise without the written permission of MATH-KNOTS LLC.

Cover Design by :
Gowri Vemuri

First Edition :
September, 2019

Author :
Gowri Vemuri

Edited by :
Ritvik Pothapragada
Siddhartha Rangavajjula
Jay Rachakonda

Questions: mathknots.help@gmail.com

NOTE : ACSL is neither affiliated nor sponsors or endorses this product.

Dedication

This book is dedicated to:

My Mom, who is my best critic, guide and supporter.

To what I am today, and what I am going to become tomorrow,

is all because of your blessings, unconditional affection and support.

This book is dedicated to the

strongest women of my life,

my dearest mom

and

to all those moms in this universe.

G.V.

ACSL

Preface

American Computer Science League (ACSL) is an international computer science competition originally founded in 1978. This organization is also an institutional member of the Computer Science Teachers Association. ACSL is on the approved activities list of the National Association of Secondary School Principals (NASSP).

ACSL consists of five divisions to appeal to the varying computing abilities and interests of students. All students at a school can take the tests but can only participate in one division. A team score is the sum of the best 3 or 5 scores in each test. Those scores can come from different students with in the team, in each contest. Prizes are awarded to top scoring students and teams based on cumulative scores after the 4th test.

The **Senior / Intermediate Division** is geared to those high school students with programming experience. Each contest consists of a 30-minute, 5- questions short answer test and a take home programming problem to be solved in 72-hours. Team scores can be based on the sum of the top 3 or top 5 scores each contest.

The **Junior Division** is geared to junior high and middle school students with no previous experience programming computers. No student beyond grade 9 may compete in the Junior Division. Each contest consists of a 30-minute 5-question short answer test and a take home program to be solved in 72-hours. Team scores are based on the sum of the best 5 scores each test.

The **Classroom Division** is open to students from all grades. It consists of a selection of the non-programming problems. As its name implies, this division is particularly well-suited for use in the classroom. Each contest consists of a 50-minute, 10-question short answer test. Team scores are based on the sum of the best 5 scores each test.

The **Elementary Division** is open to students from grades 3 - 6. It consists of non-programming problems. Four categories, one each contest, will be tested. The contest consists of a 30-minute, 5-questions test.

Preface

ELEMENTARY DIVISION	CLASS ROOM / JUNIOR DIVISION	INTERMEDIATE / SENIOR DIVISION
Elementary Computer Number Systems	Computer Number Systems	Computer Number Systems
Elementary Prefix/Infix/Postfix Notation	Recursive Functions	Recursive Functions
Elementary Boolean Algebra	What Does This Program Do? Branching	What Does This Program Do?
Elementary Graph Theory	Prefix/Infix/Postfix Notation	Prefix/Infix/Postfix Notation
	Bit-String Flicking	Bit-String Flicking
	What Does This Program Do? Loops	LISP
	Boolean Algebra	Boolean Algebra
	Data Structures	Data Structures
	What Does This Program Do? Arrays	FSA/Regular Expressions
	Graph Theory	Graph Theory
	Digital Electronics	Digital Electronics
	What Does This Program Do? Strings	Assembly Language

This book is written by computer science teachers and industry experts. Our book comprises of various practice questions in line with ACSL topics.

NOTE: ACSL is neither affiliated nor endorsed the content of this book.

This book is intended to give a hands on practice on various topics covering contest 1 and contest 2. The questions might not replicate 100% of the actual test but are intended to reinforce the basic concepts.

Index

Topic	Pages
Preface	1 - 10
Computer Number systems	11 - 40
Recursive Functions	41 - 70
What does this program do?(Branching)	71 - 100
Pre-Post/Infix Notation	101 - 132
Bit-string Flicking	133 - 166
What does this program do?(Loops)	167 - 196
Number systems Answer keys	197 - 210
Recursive Functions Answer Keys	211 - 226
What does this program do?(Branching) Answer Keys	227 - 244
Pre-Post/Infix Notation Answer Keys	245 - 260
Bit-string Flicking Answer Keys	261 - 270
What does this program do?(Loops) Answer Keys	271 - 290

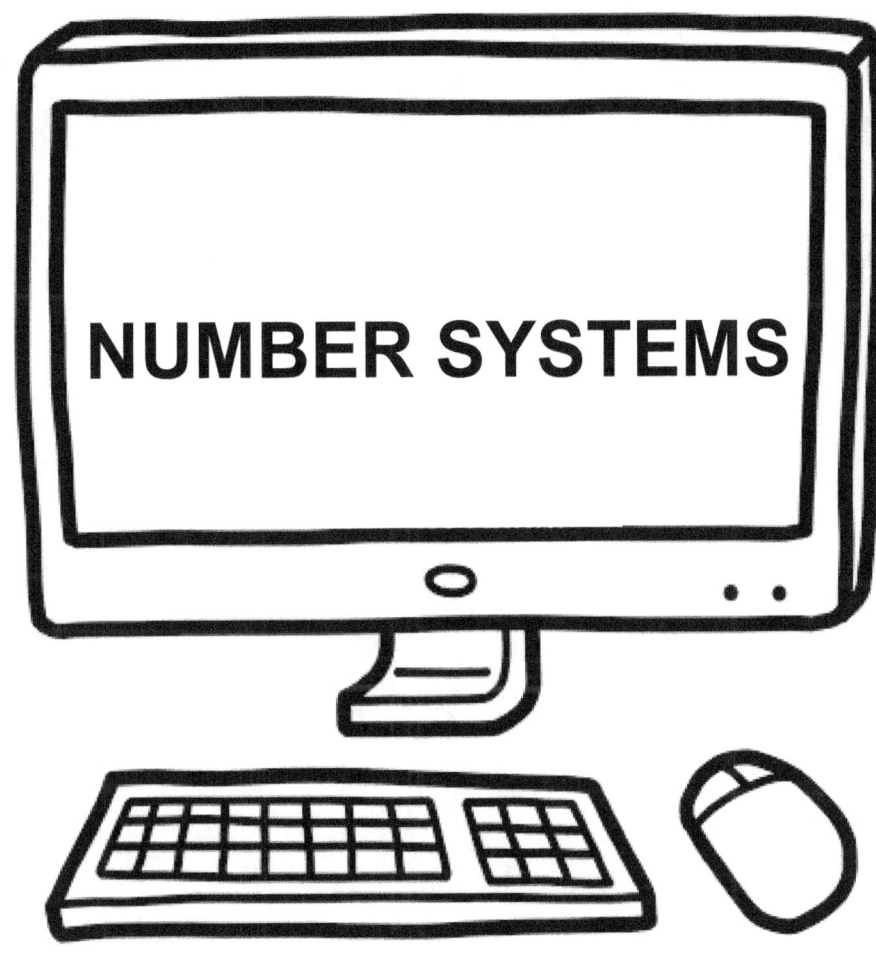

NUMBER SYSTEMS

- Decimal
- Binary
- Hexadecimal
- Octal

Decimal System:

Any number which is positionally defined in the number system is called as a decimal. All decimal numbers are with base 10.

Example: 245

$$= 2 \times 10^2 + 4 \times 10^1 + 5 \times 10^0 = 200 + 40 + 5$$

Binary System:

As the name implies binary numbers are only two : 1 and 0. All binary numbers are represented with base 2

Example: Convert the following to decimal system representation 0110100

64	32	16	8	4	2	1
0	1	1	0	1	0	0

$$= 0 \times 2^6 + 1 \times 2^5 + 1 \times 2^4 + 0 \times 2^3 + 1 \times 2^2 + 0 \times 2^1 + 0 \times 2^0$$

$$= 0 \times 64 + 1 \times 32 + 1 \times 16 + 0 \times 8 + 1 \times 4 + 0 \times 2 + 0 \times 2$$

$$= 0 + 32 + 16 + 0 + 4 + 0 + 0 = 52$$

Octa decimal System:

All octa decimal numbers are represented with base 8

Hexa decimal System:

All octa decimal numbers are represented with base 16

Comparison chart of various Number Systems

Decimal	Binary	Octal	Hexadecimal
0	0000	0	0
1	0001	1	1
2	0010	2	2
3	0011	3	3
4	0100	4	4
5	0101	5	5
6	0110	6	6
7	0111	7	7
8	1000	10	8
9	1001	11	9
10	1010	12	A
11	1011	13	B
12	1100	14	C
13	1101	15	D
14	1110	16	E
15	1111	17	F

TEST 1

1. Convert the following to decimal system representation.
   100111

2. Convert the following to decimal system representation:
   101110

3. Convert the following to decimal system representation:
1011111

4. Convert the following to decimal system representation:
0011111

5. Convert the following to decimal system representation:
1011010

6. Convert the following to binary system representation:
30

7. Convert the following to binary system representation:
45

8. Solve A - 50 = 10 and represent the answer in binary representation.

9. Convert the following to binary system representation:
   69

10. Convert the following to binary system representation:
    100

11. Convert the following to decimal system representation:
    101100 + 101001

12. Solve A - 25 = 15 and represent the answer in binary representation.
    A = 40

13. Convert the following to binary system representation:
    28

14. Solve A + 10 = 30 and represent the answer in binary representation.
    A = 20

15. Convert the following to decimal system representation:
    101001 - 000011

16. Convert the following to decimal system representation:
    11101 + 10001

17. Solve $x_8 = 1011$ $y_8 = 1000\ 0001$. Find $x_8 + y_8$

18. Convert the following to decimal system representation:
    111101 + 101010

19. Convert the following to decimal system representation:
101101 + 001010

20. Solve $A_8 = 0001\ 0001$ $B_8 = 1100\ 0001.$ Find $A_8 + B_8$

21. Convert the following to decimal system representation:
    101101 + 001011

22. Convert the following to decimal system representation:
    1101001 - 0000111

23. Convert 0xA6 to binary.

24. If $A_8 = 0010\ 0100$ $B_8 = 1001\ 0000.$ Find $A_8 + B_8$

25. Convert 0XB 7 to binary.

26. Add 0xA4 and 0xC3 by converting into decimal.

27. Convert 232 into hexadecimal.

28. Solve $A_8 = 1001\ 0001$ $B_8 = 0100\ 0001.$ Find $A_8 - B_8$

29. Add 0xD8 and 0xA9 by converting into decimal.

30. Convert 0xE2 to binary and then convert the binary to decimal.

31. If $A_8 = 100\ 001$ $B_8 = 0001\ 1000$. Find $A_8 + B_8$

32. Convert the following to decimal system representation:
    010101 + 101011

33. Convert 167 into hexadecimal.

34. Solve $A_8 = 1000\ 1001$ $B_8 = 0110\ 0001$. Find $A_8 - B_8$

35. Solve 0XD4 - 0XAA by converting into decimal

36. Convert 245 into hexadecimal.

37. Solve 0xAD2 – 0xA2B by converting into decimal.

38. Convert 250 into hexadecimal.

39. Solve 0xAC3 – 0xA2 by converting into decimal.

40. Add 0xA9 and 0xE5 by converting into decimal.

41. Convert 120 into hexadecimal.

42. Solve $A_8 = 0001\ 1000\ 0001$ $B_8 = 1000\ 0001$. Find $A_8 - B_8$

43. Convert 340 into hexadecimal.

44. Convert 340 into hexadecimal.

45. Solve $A_8 = 0001\ 0001\ 0001$ $B_8 = 0101\ 0001.$ Find $A_8 - B_8$

46. Convert the following to decimal system representation:
    100101 + 101000

47. Convert 0xB7A to binary.

48. Convert 350 into hexadecimal.

49. Convert the following to decimal system representation:
    101111 - 101000

50. Solve $A_8 = 0001\ 0000\ 0011$ $B_8 = 0001\ 0000\ 0001.$ Find $A_8 - B_8$

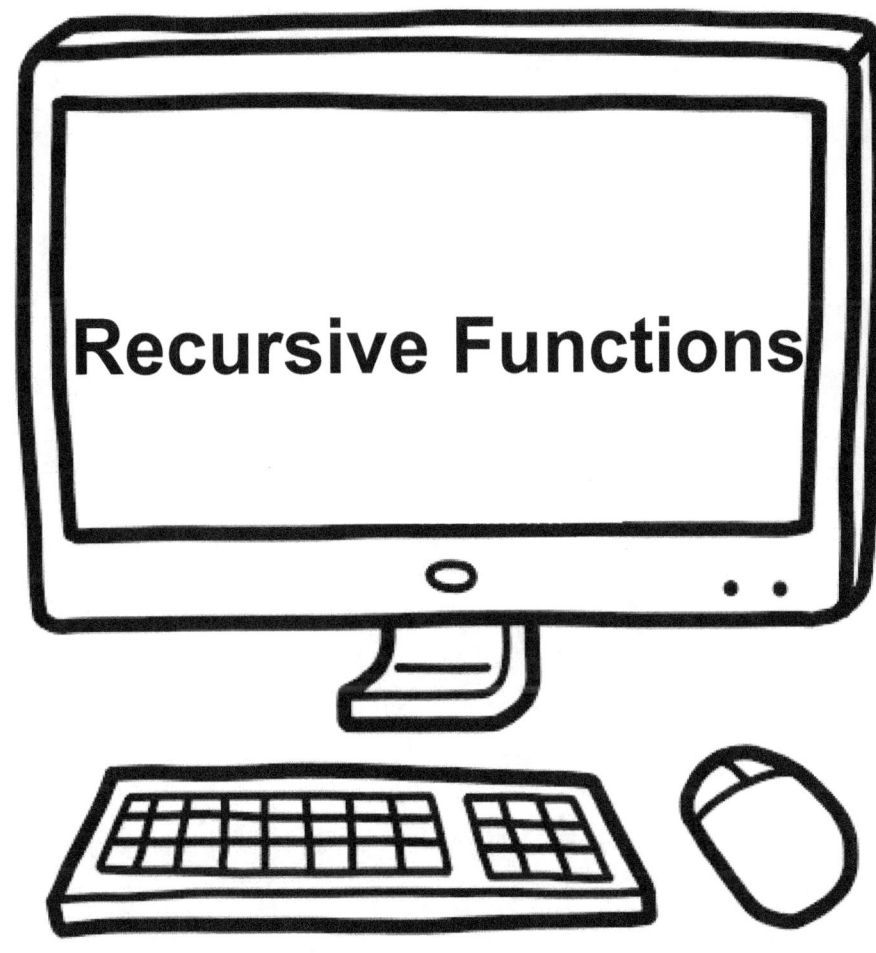

Recursive Functions

As the name says it is characterized by recurrence or repetition. This involves the repeated application of a rule, formula or a procedure based on certain given conditions to obtain successive results. These functions are widely used in programs or routines of which a part requires the application of the whole, so that its explicit call requires in general many successive executions.

Example: Any arithmetic sequence, Fibonacci numbers is a good example of recursive functions.

Sample Problem:

Find $f(5,4)$

$$f(x,y) = \begin{cases} f(x, y+1) & \text{when } x > y \\ f(x+1, y+2) & \text{when } x < y \\ -2x + \dfrac{y}{x} + xy & \text{when } x = y \end{cases}$$

Step 1:
$f(x,y) = f(5,4)$ x = 5 and y = 4 ; x > y

$f(x, y+1) = f(5, 4+1) = f(5,5)$

Step 2:
$f(x,y) = f(5,5)$ x = 5 and y = 5 ; x = y

$f(5,5) =$
$= -2(5) + \dfrac{5}{5} + (5)(5)$
$= -10 + 1 + 25 = 16$

ACSL
Recursive functions

TEST 1

1. Evaluate the following recursive functions:
   Find $f(5,3)$

   $$f(x,y) = \begin{cases} f(x-1, y) & \text{when } x > y \\ x - y & \text{otherwise} \end{cases}$$

2. Find $f(8,2)$

   $$f(x,y) = \begin{cases} f(x-2, y+1) & \text{when } x > y \\ x + y & \text{otherwise} \end{cases}$$

TEST 1

3. Find $f(9,5)$

$$f(x,y) = \begin{cases} f(x-y, y+1) & \text{when } x > y \\ x+y & \text{otherwise} \end{cases}$$

4. Find $f(20,5)$

$$f(x,y) = \begin{cases} f(f(x-y, y+1)) & \text{when } x > y \\ x+y & \text{otherwise} \\ 1 & 0 \le x \le 10, y = non-existent \\ 0 & x > 10, y = non-existent \end{cases}$$

TEST 1

5. Find $f(8,5)$

$$f(x,y) = \begin{cases} f(f(x,y+1)) & \text{when } x > y \\ x + \dfrac{y}{x} & \text{otherwise} \\ 5 & 0 \leq x \leq 10, y = non - existent \\ 10 & x > 10, y = non - existent \end{cases}$$

6. Find $f(9,11)$

$$f(x,y) = \begin{cases} f(f(x,y-x)) & \text{when } x < y \\ x + \dfrac{x}{y} & \text{otherwise} \\ 0 & 0 \leq x \leq 5, y = non - existent \\ 1 & x > 5, y = non - existent \end{cases}$$

7. Find $f(4,10)$

$$f(x,y) = \begin{cases} (f(x, y-x)) & \text{when } x < y \\ f(x-1, y+1) & \text{when } x > y \\ x+y & \text{otherwise} \end{cases}$$

8. Find $f(10,8)$

$$f(x,y) = \begin{cases} f(x-1, y+2) & \text{when } x > y \\ x + \dfrac{y}{x^{\frac{1}{2}}} & \text{otherwise} \end{cases}$$

9. Find $f(5)$

$$f(x) = \begin{cases} f(x-2) + 2 & \text{when } x > 2 \\ 0 & x = 1 \\ 1 & x = 2 \end{cases}$$

10. Find $f(5)$ if $f(x) = 3 \cdot f(x-2) + 3$ and we know that $f(1) = 10$

ACSL
Recursive functions

TEST 1

11. Evaluate the following recursive functions:
Find $f(3)$

$$f(x) = \begin{cases} f(x-1) - 1 & \text{when } x > 1 \\ 0 & x = 1 \\ 1 & x = 0 \end{cases}$$

12. Find $f(4,2)$

$$f(x,y) = \begin{cases} f\left(x - \frac{3}{2}, y - 1\right) & \text{when } x > y \\ x + \frac{y}{x^2} & \text{otherwise} \end{cases}$$

ACSL
Recursive functions

TEST 1

11. Evaluate the following recursive functions:
Find $f(3)$

$$f(x) = \begin{cases} f(x-1) - 1 & \text{when } x > 1 \\ 0 & x = 1 \\ 1 & x = 0 \end{cases}$$

12. Find $f(4,2)$

$$f(x,y) = \begin{cases} f\left(x - \dfrac{3}{2}, y - 1\right) & \text{when } x > y \\ x + \dfrac{y}{x^2} & \text{otherwise} \end{cases}$$

13. Find $f(4,5)$

$$f(x,y) = \begin{cases} f(x+y, y-1^3) & \text{when } x < y \\ x+y & x = \text{even} \\ x-y & x = \text{odd} \end{cases}$$

14. Find $f(4,8)$

$$f(x,y) = \begin{cases} (f(x+1, y-2)) & \text{when } x < y \\ x+y & \text{otherwise} \end{cases}$$

TEST 1

15. Find $f(7,5)$

$$f(x,y) = \begin{cases} f(f(x-1, y+\frac{3}{2})) & \text{when } x > y \\ x - \frac{y}{x}, y & \text{otherwise} \end{cases}$$

Subject to conditions $f(x,y) = x + y$, for $y - x \geq 2.5$

16. Find $f(9,4)$

$$f(x,y) = \begin{cases} f(f(x, y^2 - 4)) & \text{when } x > y \\ x + \frac{2x}{4y} & \text{otherwise} \\ 1 & x > 5 \text{ and } y \text{ is non} - existent \end{cases}$$

17. Find $f(2,8)$

$$f(x,y) = \begin{cases} f(x+y, y-1) & \text{when } x < y \\ f(x-3, y) & \text{when } x > y \\ x + \dfrac{y}{x^2} & \text{otherwise} \end{cases}$$

18. Find $f(a,b)$ where $a > b$ and $a - b = 1$

$$f(x,y) = \begin{cases} f(x-2, y+2) & \text{when } x > y \\ x + \dfrac{y}{x^{\frac{1}{2}}} & \text{otherwise} \end{cases}$$

19. Find $f(a)$ where is the biggest even number ranging between 1 and 10

$$f(x) = \begin{cases} f(x-2) + 2 & \text{when } x > 2 \\ 0 & x = 1, 0 \\ 1 & x = 2 \end{cases}$$

20. Find $f\left(49^{\frac{1}{2}}\right)$

$$f(x) = \begin{cases} f(x-2) + x & \text{when } x > 2 \\ 0 & x = 1, 0 \\ 1 & x = 2 \end{cases}$$

TEST 1

21. Evaluate the following recursive functions:

$$f(x) = \begin{cases} \text{Find } f(5) & \\ f(x-1) - \dfrac{1}{2} & \text{when } x > 1 \\ -1 & x = 1 \\ 1 & x = 0 \\ 0 & x = 2 \end{cases}$$

Write the complete series in the end.

22. Find $f(6,2)$

$$f(x,y) = \begin{cases} f(\dfrac{x}{y}, y) & \text{when } x > y \\ x + \dfrac{y}{x^2} & \text{otherwise} \end{cases}$$

TEST 1

23. Find $f(3,6)$

$$f(x,y) = \begin{cases} f(f(x+y,y)) & \text{when } x < y \\ x - y & \text{otherwise} \\ 0 & 1 \leq x \leq 10, y = non-existent \end{cases}$$

24. Find $f(a,b)$ where $a > b$ and $a = b - a$

$$f(x,y) = \begin{cases} f(x, y+a) & \text{when } x < y \\ x + y & \text{otherwise} \end{cases}$$

TEST 1

25. Find $f(8,6)$

$$f(x,y) = \begin{cases} f(x-y, y) & \text{when } x > y \\ x - \dfrac{y}{x} & \text{otherwise} \end{cases}$$

26. Find $f(5,4)$

$$f(x,y) = \begin{cases} f(f(x-1, y+4)) & \text{when } x > y \\ x + \dfrac{2x}{4y} & \text{otherwise} \\ 1 & x > 5 \text{ and } y \text{ is non} - \text{existent} \\ 0 & x < 5 \text{ and } y \text{ is non} - \text{existent} \end{cases}$$

27. Find $f(1,6)$

$$(x,y) = \begin{cases} f(2x, y-1) & \text{when } x < y \\ f(x+3, \frac{y}{6}) & \text{when } x > y \\ x + \frac{y}{x^2} & \text{otherwise} \end{cases}$$

28. Find $f(7,4)$

$$(x,y) = \begin{cases} f(x-2, y+2) & \text{when } x > y \\ x + y^2 & \text{otherwise} \end{cases}$$

29. Find $f(5)$

$$(x,y) = \begin{cases} f(x-2) + x & \text{when } x > 1 \\ 0 & x = 1, 0 \end{cases}$$

30. Find $f(4)$

$$f(x) = \begin{cases} f(x + x^2) & \text{when } x > 2 \\ 4 & x = 1, 0 \\ -2 & x = 2 \end{cases}$$

31. Evaluate the following recursive functions:

$$a(x) = \begin{cases} \text{Find } a(4) \\ a(1) = -4 \\ a(n) = a(n-1) + 4 \end{cases}$$

32. Find $a(5)$

$$a(x) = \begin{cases} a(0) = 2 \\ a(1) = 1 \\ a(n) = a(n-2) + n \end{cases}$$

33. Find $C(5)$

$$C(x) = \begin{cases} C(0) = a \\ C(1) = b \\ C(n) = C(n-1) + 2 \end{cases}$$

34. Find $C(6)$

$$C(x) = \begin{cases} C(0) = \dfrac{a}{2} \\ C(1) = b \\ C(n) = C(n-2) + n \end{cases}$$

35. Find $f(4)$

$$f(x) = \begin{cases} f(f(x-1)) & x > 1 \\ 1 & x = 1 \end{cases}$$

36. Find $f(4)$

$$f(x) = \begin{cases} f(x-1) + a & x > 1 \\ 0 & x = 1 \end{cases}$$

37. Complete the missing values in the recursive formula of the sequence: 2, 8, 14, ...

$$\begin{cases} a(1) = A \\ a(n) = e(n-1) + B \\ A = ?, B = ? \end{cases}$$

38. Complete the missing values in the recursive formula of the sequence: -1, -4, -7, ...

$$\begin{cases} a(1) = A \\ a(n) = e(n-1) + B \\ A = ?, B = ? \end{cases}$$

ACSL
Recursive functions
TEST 1

39. Find $f(5)$

$$f(n) = \begin{cases} f(n-2) + \dfrac{n}{2} & n > 3 \\ 1 & n = 1 \\ 0 & n = 0 \end{cases}$$

40. Find $f(a,b)$ where $a > b$ and $a = b - a$

$$f(x,y) = \begin{cases} f(\dfrac{x}{2}, \dfrac{y}{8} + \dfrac{a}{2}) & \text{when } x < y \\ x + \dfrac{y}{2} & \text{otherwise} \end{cases}$$

41. Evaluate the following recursive function and add Find $f(8,6)$

$$f(x,y) = \begin{cases} f(x-1, y) & \text{when } x > y \\ x - \sqrt{y} & \text{otherwise} \end{cases}$$

42. Find $f(6,3)$

$$f(x,y) = \begin{cases} f(x-1, y+1) & \text{when } x > y \\ x + \left(\dfrac{2x}{4y}\right)^{\frac{1}{2}} & \text{otherwise} \end{cases}$$

TEST 1

43. Find $f(3,6)$

$$f(x,y) = \begin{cases} f(3x, y) & \text{when } x < y \\ f(x, y+3) & \text{when } x > y \\ x + \dfrac{yx}{x^{\frac{1}{2}}} & \text{otherwise} \end{cases}$$

44. Find $f(4)$

$$f(x) = \begin{cases} f(x-1) - (x^2) & \text{when } x > 1 \\ 1 & x = 1 \\ -2 & x = 0 \\ 0 & x = 2 \end{cases}$$

45. Find $f(12,3)$

$$f(x,y) = \begin{cases} f(\frac{x}{3}, y) & \text{when } x > y \\ f(x+1.7, y) & x < y \\ x + yx & x = y \end{cases}$$

46. Find $f(2,4)$

$$f(x,y) = \begin{cases} f(x+y, \frac{y}{x}) & \text{when } x < y \\ f(x, y+4) & x > y \\ x + \frac{y}{x} + xy & x = y \end{cases}$$

47. Find $f(3)$

$$f(x) = \begin{cases} f(1) = 1 \\ f(x) = f(x-1) + \dfrac{1}{x} \end{cases}$$

48. Find $a(4)$

$$a(n) = \begin{cases} a(0) = -2 \\ a(1) = -3 \\ a(n) = a(n-2) + n^2 \end{cases}$$

49. Find $a(5)$

$$a(x) = \begin{cases} a = 0 & \text{at } x = 0 \\ a = 1 & \text{at } x = 1 \\ a(x) = a(x-2) + \dfrac{x+1}{2} & \text{at other values of } x \end{cases}$$

50. Evaluate the following recursive functions:

$$f(x,y) = \begin{cases} \text{Find } f(6,3) & \\ f\left(x - \dfrac{1}{2}, y\right) & \text{when } x > y \\ x - \dfrac{y}{xy} & \text{otherwise} \end{cases}$$

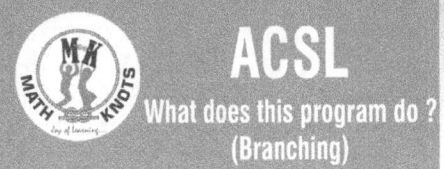

What does this program do ?

Students are given small code snippets to understand and analyze the programming concepts. The goal is to get them familiarize to understand and debug the software programs written in any language.

Four concepts are emphasized as below

- Looping
- Branching
- Arrays
- Strings

1. What is the output of the program?
b=-1;
if(b<0)
Output "The value is negative"
else Output "The value is positive"

2. What is the output of the program?
b= 0
if(b<0)
Output "The value is negative"
elseif (b>0)
Output "The value is positive"
else
Output "The value is the smallest whole number"

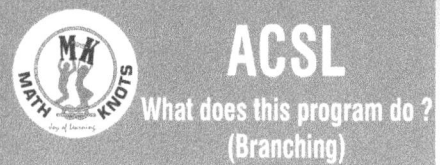

3. What is the output of the program?
a= 5
b=5
if (a==b)
Output "True"

4. What is the output of the program if you enter A?
A=3
B=5
if (A==B)
Output "True"
else
Output "False"

5. What is the output of the program?
```
c = 0
while c< 8
output (c)
if c==4
break
c+=1
```

6. What is the output of the program?
```
A = 0
for B = 7 to 21 step 7
A = A + B
next B
end
```

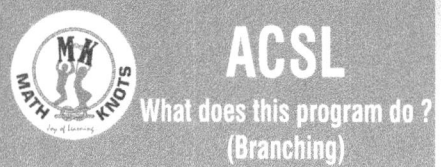

7. What is the output of the program?
a=2
b=4
c = 0
d = 3
if a<b
   c=a+b
   d = c+b
   Output d
end

8. What is the output of the program?
a=8
b=4
c = 0
d = 0
if a>b
   c=a-b
   d = c+a
   Output d
end

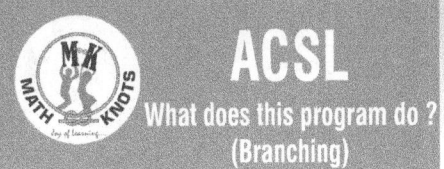

9. What is the output of the program?
```
a=5
b=3
c = 0
d = 0
if a>b
   c=a+b
   d = c+a
   Output d
end
```

10. What is the output of the program?
```
a=5
b=3
c =0
d =0
e=0
f=0
if a>b
   c=a+b
   d = c+a
   e=b+c
   f=d+e
end
Output f
```

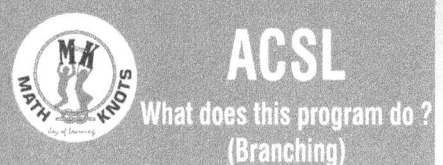

11. What is the output of the program?
```
a=5
b=3
c =0
d =0
e=0
f=0
if a>b && b>c
    c=a+b
    d = c-a
    e=b+c
    f=d+e
end
Output f
```

12. What is the output of the program?
```
a=5
 for i= 1:10
   c=a+i
   if c>11
      break
   end
   Output c

end
```

13. What is the output of the program?
```
a=4
for i= 1:2:12
   c=a+i
   if c>12
      break
   end
Output c

end
```

14. What is the output of the program?
```
a=4
b=2
for i= 1:2:12
   c=a+i
   d=c+b
   if c>11
      break
   end
   Output d

end
```

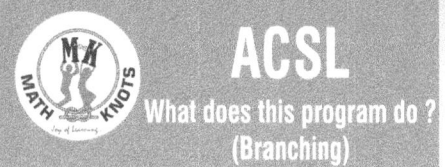

15. What is the output of the program?
a=3
b=3

for i= 1:2:12
  c=a+i
  d=c+b
  e=d+d
  Output e

end

16. What is the final output of the program?
a=2
b=3
for i= 1:2:12
  c=a+i
  d=c+b
  e=d+d
  Output e
end

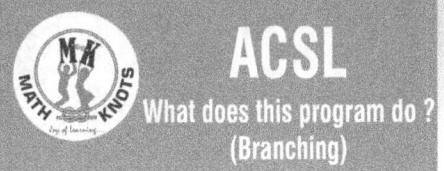

17. What is the output of the program?
```
a=2
b=3
for i= 1:2:12
   c=b+i
   d=c+b
   e=d+b
  Output e
end
```

18. What is the output of the program?
```
a=5
b=3
c = 0
d = 0
if a>b
   c=a+b
   a=10
   d = c+a
   Output d
else
Output "1"
end
```

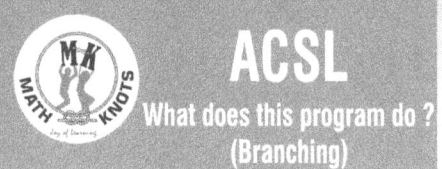

19. What is the value of "g"?
a=5
b=3
c = 0
d = 0
if a>b
   c=a+b
   a=10
   d = c+a
else
break
end
f=12
g=d+f
Output g

20. What is the value of "g"?
a=2
b=3
c = 0
d = 0
if a<b
   c=a+b
   a=10
   d = c+a
else
break;
end
f=10
g=d+f
Output g

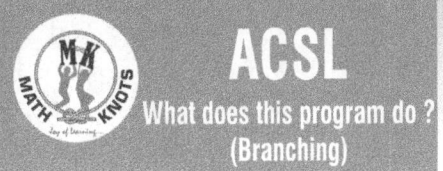

21. What is the output?
```
a=2
b=3
c = 0
d = 0
if a<b
   c=a+b
   a=c
   d = c+a

end
f=10
g=d+f
```

22. What is the output of the program if the user enters 10?
```
t = 50
s=10
if t>s
   Output "smaller"
elseif Output "larger"
else
   Output "error"
end
```

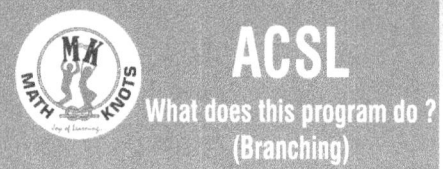

23. What is the value of a after the execution of the statement if a = 10 and b = 20?
a= (a <b) ? b : -b

24. What is the value of a after the execution of the statement if a = 45 and b = 35?
a= (a <b) ? b : -b

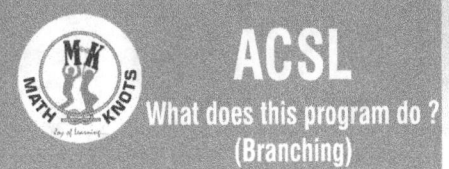

25. What is the output of the program if n = 10?
n= 10
if(n%2 == 0)
Output "even"
else
Output "odd"

26. What is the output of the program if n = 19?
n= 19
if(n%2 == 0)
Output "even"
else
Output "odd"

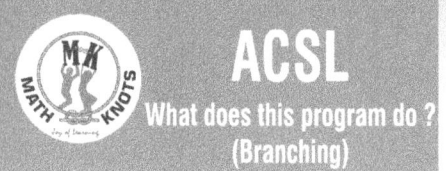

27. What is the output of the statement if n = 144?
(n % 2 ==0) ? Output << n << "is even" : Output<< n << "is odd";

28. What is the output of the program?
n=8
i = true;
for (i=2; i<=n, ++i)
if (n% i==0)
iprime=false
Output "No"
break;
else
Output "Yes"

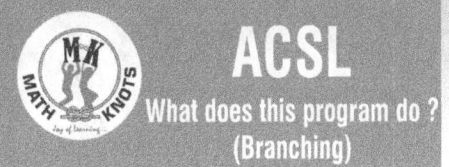

29. What is the output of the program if n = 10?
```
n = 10
for(i=1; i<=n; ++i)
if(n%i==0)
Output i
```

30. What is the output of the program?
```
int n=45, i;
 bool i = true;
for (i=2; i<=n, ++i)
 If (n % i==0)
 i = false;
 Output "No"
 break;
else
Output "Yes"
```

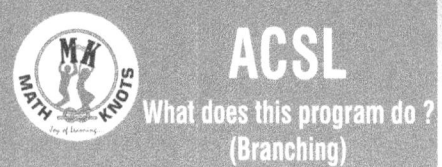

31. What is the output of the statement?
int n=40
if(n%2 == 0)
Output "Yes"
else
Output "No"

32. What is the output of the statement?
int n = 31;
(n%2==0) ? Output<< n << " Yes" : Output << n << "No";

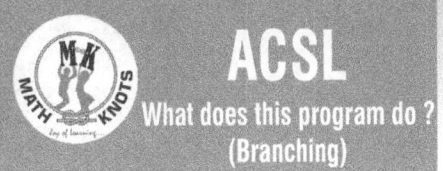

33. What is the output of the program?
```
int n = 10
int add(int n)
if (n!=0)
return n + add(n-1)
```

34. What is the output of the program?
```
int n=40
if(n/2 == 0)
Output "Yes"
else
Output "No"
```

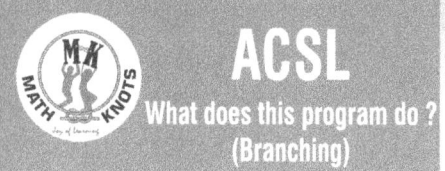

35. What is the output of the program if n = 10 and m = 12?
int n=10, m=12
if (n>m)
Output "n is larger"
else
Output "m is larger"

36. What is the output of the program?

t = 50 ;
s = 50
if t>s
   Output "smaller"
elseif t<s
Output "larger"
else
   Output "error"
end

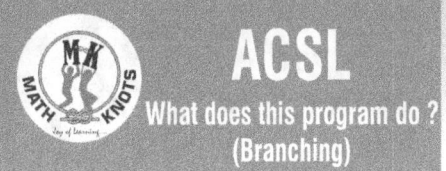

37. What is the output of the program if n= 12, m = 1, a = 15?
int n, m, a;
if (n>m && n>a)
{
Output "n"
elseif (m>n && m>a)
Output "m"
else
Output "a"

38. What is the output of the program?
int n = 3995;
(n%2==0) ? Output << n << " Yes" : Output << n << "No";

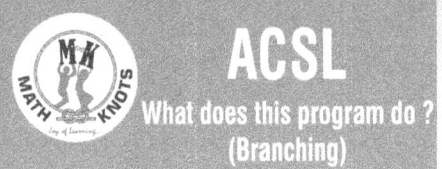

39. What is the output of the program n=1, m = 2, a =2?
int n, m, a
if (n>m && n>a)
{
Output "n"
elseif (m>n && m>a)
Output "m"
else
Output "a"

40. What is the output of the program a=2, c=-2?
a= (a <c) ? -c : c ;

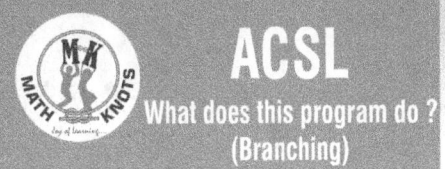

41. What is the output of the program?
```
int n = 6
Output (factorial(n))
int factorial (int n)
   if(n > 1)
      return n * factorial(n - 1);
   else
      return 1;
```

42. What is the output of the program?
```
score = 90
if (score == 100)
grade = 'A';
Output "A"
else if (score >= 90)
grade = 'A'
Output "Excellent"
else if (score >= 80)
grade = 'B'
Output "B"
else if (score >= 70)
grade = 'C'
Output "Good"
else if (score >= 60)
grade = 'D'
else
grade = 'F'
```

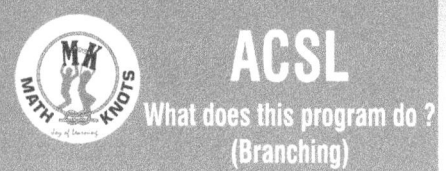

43. What is the output of the program?
age = 20, height = 170
if(height == age)
   Output "Equal !"
else if(height < age)
   Output "Height!"
else if(height > age
   Output "Age!"

44. What is the output of the program?
   int age =40
   if(age >= 35 && age <= 80)
     Output "You're between 35 and 80 and cannot save money on your health insurance!"
   else
     Output "Contact the office, we may have deals for you"

45. What is the output of the program if age=45?
    ```
    int age;
    output "Enter your age: "
    if (age < 0 || age > 200)
       Output "Error."
    else
       Output "Age entered"
    ```

46. What is the output of the program if x=8?
    ```
    if (x > 0)
      Output  "positive"
    else if (x < 0)
      Output "negative"
    else
      Output  "zero"
    ```

47. What is the output of the program?
   int num=9;
   if(num == 1)
      Output "The number is 1"
   else if(num == 2)
      Output "The number is 2"
   else
      Output "The number is not 1 or 2"

48. What is the output of the program?
   int a = 100;
   if(a == 20)
      Output "a is 20"
   else if(a == 40)
      Output "a is 40"
   else if(a == 60)
      Output "a is 60"
   else
      Output "a does not match"
   Output a

49. What is the output of the program?
```
   int a = 20;
   if( a == 20 )
      Output "a is 20"
else if( a == 40 )
      Output "a is 40"
else if( a == 60 )
      Output "a is 60"
else
      Output "a does not match"
   Output a
```

50. What is the output of the program if n1=2 and n2=5?
```
   n1=2 and n2=5
   m = (n1 > n2) ? n1 : n2;
   do
      if (m % n1 == 0 && m % n2 == 0)
         Output m
         break;
      else
         ++m;
   while (true);
```

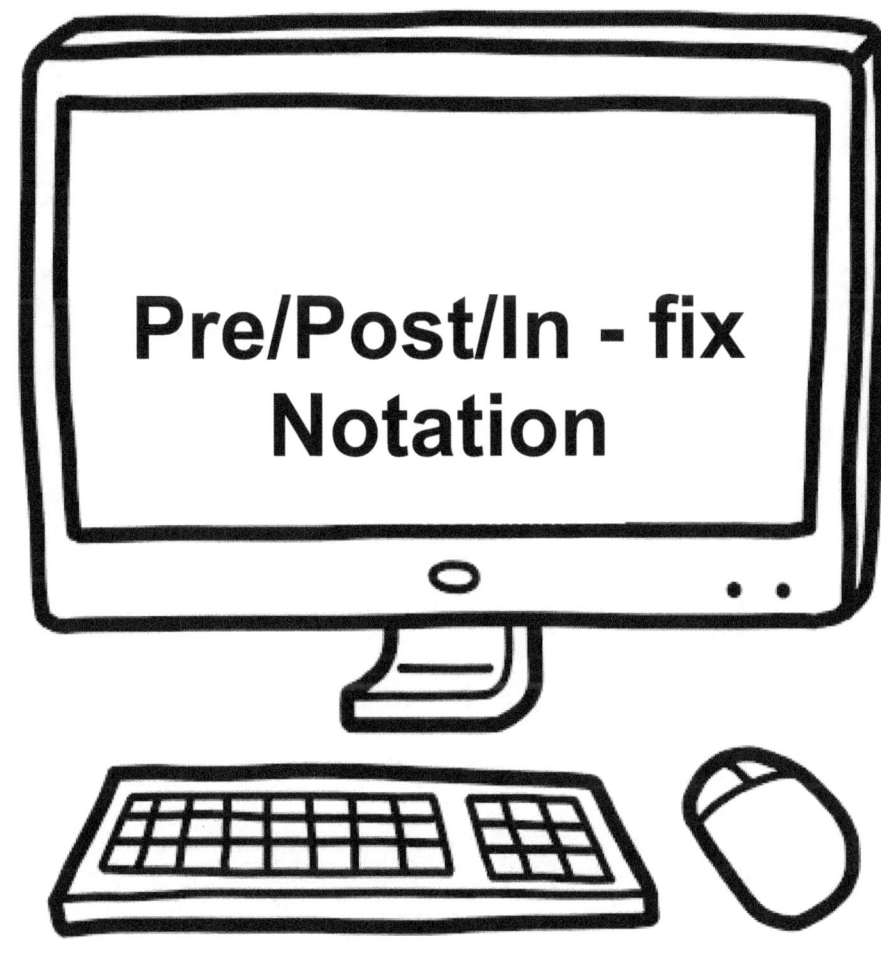

Prefix-Postfix Notations

Infix Notation:

P + Q

As a general way of writing expressions, Operators are written in-between their operands.

An expression such as A *(B + C) /D

is simplified as "First add B and C together, then multiply the result by A, then divide by D."

The Infix Notations use the general order of evaluation, using PEDMAS rules

Prefix Notation:

Infix, Postfix and Prefix notations are three different but equivalent ways of writing expressions. It is easiest to demonstrate the differences by looking at examples of operators that take two operands.

Infix notation: A + B.   Prefix notation: + X Y

Operators are written before their operands.

An expression such as A *(B + C) /D = / (A *(B + C)) D

= / * A(B+C) D /= / * A + B C D

- The order of evaluation of operators is always left-to-right Brackets cannot be used to change this order.
- Because the "/" is to the left of the "*" in the example above, the addition must be performed before the multiplication.
- Operators act on values immediately to the left of them. For example, the "+" above uses the "B" and "C".
- Brackets can be added to make this more explicit
   (/ (* A (+ B C)) D)

SAMPLE #1:

Convert the following infix to prefix notation:

$$(A - D) + \frac{B}{C}$$

$$= ((A - D)) + (\frac{B}{C})$$

$$= ((-AD)) + (\frac{B}{C})$$

$$= (-AD) + (/BC)$$

$$= + - AD/BC$$

Postfix Notation:

Infix notation: A + B
Postfix notation (also known as "Reverse Polish notation"): A B +

    Operators are written after their operands.

    An expression such as A *(B + C) /D = A *(B + C) D /

$$= A(B+C) *D / = A B C + * D /$$

- The order of evaluation of operators is always left-to-right
- Brackets cannot be used to change this order.
- Because the "+" is to the left of the "*" in the example above, the addition must be performed before the multiplication.
- Operators act on values immediately to the left of them. For example, the "+" above uses the "B" and "C".
- Brackets can be added to make this more explicit
  ((A (B C +) *) D /)

Thus, the "*" uses the two values immediately preceding: "A", and the result of the addition. Similarly, the "/" uses the result of the multiplication and the "D".

In all notations, the operands occur in the same order, and just the operators have to be moved to keep the meaning correct.

SAMPLE #2:

Convert the following infix into postfix notations:

$$\frac{A + B + C + A^2}{4}$$

$$= \frac{((A + B + C) + A^2)}{4}$$

$$= \frac{((AB + C) + A^2)}{4}$$

$$= \frac{(ABC + A2\uparrow +)}{4}$$

$$= ABC + A2\uparrow +4/$$

ACSL
Pre/Post/In - fix Notation

Test 2

1. Convert the following infix into prefix notations

$$A * \frac{B}{C} + D$$

2. Convert the following infix to prefix notation:

$$A + B * C + D^E + E^D$$

3. Convert the following infix to prefix notation:

$$(A * B) + (C * \frac{A}{B})$$

4. Convert the following infix into postfix notations:

$$\frac{A + B + A^2 + B^2}{3}$$

5. Convert the following infix into postfix notation:
$$A * B * (C - B) * (D - A)$$

6. Convert the following prefix into infix notation
$$- * + ABB \uparrow C2$$

7. Convert the following infix into prefix notation:
$$\frac{A-B}{C-D} + \frac{A^B}{C^D}$$

8. Convert the following infix to postfix notation:
$$A * B + C * A - B$$

9. Convert the following infix to postfix notation:

$$\left(\frac{D}{C} + \frac{C}{B} + \frac{B}{A}\right)^E$$

10. Convert the following infix to prefix notations:

$$(A - B) + \frac{C - D}{B}$$

11. Convert the following infix to prefix notation:
$$A * B + (A + B) + A^B$$

12. Convert the following infix to postfix notation:
$$A * D * E * (A - C)$$

13. Convert the following infix to postfix notations:

$$\frac{(A - \frac{B}{C})}{B - C}$$

14. Convert the following infix to prefix notation:

$$(A - D) * (D - A) + \frac{B}{C}$$

15. Convert the following infix to postfix notation:
$$(A^2 + B^3 + (A - B)^4)$$

16. Convert the following prefix into infix notation:
$$+ - AB * \frac{C}{DA}, where\ A = B = 2, C = D = 3$$

17. Convert the following infix to prefix notation:

$$\frac{A-B}{C} + \frac{C}{A-B}$$

18. Convert the following infix notations into prefix notation:

$$A^{A^A} + \frac{B}{\frac{B}{B}}$$

19. Convert the following infix notations into prefix notation:
$$A - B^3 + \frac{C}{D^2}$$

20. Convert the following prefix to infix notation:
$$+ - A C * A / C B$$

21. Convert the following infix to postfix notation:

$$A - \frac{B}{B} + \frac{B^2}{B^2} + A$$

22. Convert the following infix notation to post fix notation:

$$(A - B) * (B - \frac{C}{D})$$

23. Convert the following infix to prefix notation:
$$\frac{A}{A-C} + B * (C - D)$$

24. Convert the following infix to postfix notation:
$$A - B + \frac{C}{D}$$

25. Convert the following infix into prefix notation:

$$A * B * \frac{C}{D} * A$$

26. Convert the following infix into postfix notation

$$(A - B) + (\frac{A}{B})^2$$

27. Convert the following infix to prefix notation:
$$(A - B)^2 + (B * C)^3$$

28. Convert the following infix to prefix notation:
$$A - [\frac{B + C}{D}]^2 + (A * C)$$

29. Convert the following infix to prefix notation:
$$A * C^3 + D^4 + C^2 * D$$

30. Convert the following infix to postfix notation:
$$\frac{A+B}{A-C} + C - D$$

31. Convert the following infix to prefix notation:
$$\left[\frac{A+B}{A+C}\right]^E * \left[\frac{C*D}{C*B}\right]^F$$

32. Convert the following postfix to infix notation and find the final answer:
$$AB * G \uparrow BC/F \uparrow +CD/E \uparrow +$$
where $A = C = 88;\ B = D = 90;\ E = F = G = 0$

33. Convert the following infix to prefix notations:
$$A + \frac{A}{B} + \frac{B}{A} * A$$

34. Convert the following infix to postfix notation:
$$\frac{A-B}{B^2} + \frac{C-D}{C^3}$$

35. Convert the following postfix to infix notation and find the final answer:

$$AB \uparrow 2 - \frac{CD}{+}, \text{where } A = B = 2; C = D = -2$$

36. Convert the following infix to prefix notation:

$$\frac{A-B}{B-A} + (A^B * B^A)$$

37. Convert the following infix to postfix notation:
$$\frac{C}{D} + A^2 + B^3$$

38. Convert the following infix to prefix notation:
$$A^A * \frac{A^A}{B^B}$$

39. Convert the following infix to postfix notation:

$$A * B + B + A - \frac{C^C}{A - C}$$

40. Convert the following infix to postfix notation:

$$\left[\frac{A+B}{A}\right]^2 * \left[\frac{C-D}{C}\right]^3$$

41. Convert the following infix to prefix notation:
$$\frac{A-B}{A^2-B^2} + C^3 - \frac{D^2}{A^2}$$

42. Convert the following infix to postfix notation:
$$(A - B^3 + \frac{C^4}{A^3} + (B*C))$$

43. Convert the following infix to prefix notations:
$$A^2 - \left[\frac{B+C}{D^2}\right]^2 + (A*C)^2$$

44. Convert the following infix to postfix notation:
$$X^2 + \frac{Y^X}{X^3} - \frac{Y-X}{X*Y}$$

45. Convert the following postfix to infix notation and evaluate the final answer:
$$23/4 + 45/-42\uparrow-$$

46. Evaluate "S" in prefix form:
$$S = \frac{P^2}{Q^3} + \frac{(P-Q)}{P^R}$$

47. Convert the following infix to postfix notation:
$$O^T - \frac{P^S}{P^P} + (O - P), where\ T = 2\ and\ S = 3$$

48. Convert the following prefix to infix notation:
$$-+/25/43-43$$

49. Convert the following infix to prefix notation:

$$\frac{(\frac{A-C}{A+C})}{\frac{A}{C}}$$

50. Evaluate the expression for "R" in postfix form:

$$R = \frac{(\frac{P-Q^2}{P^2+Q})}{(P-\frac{Q}{2})}$$

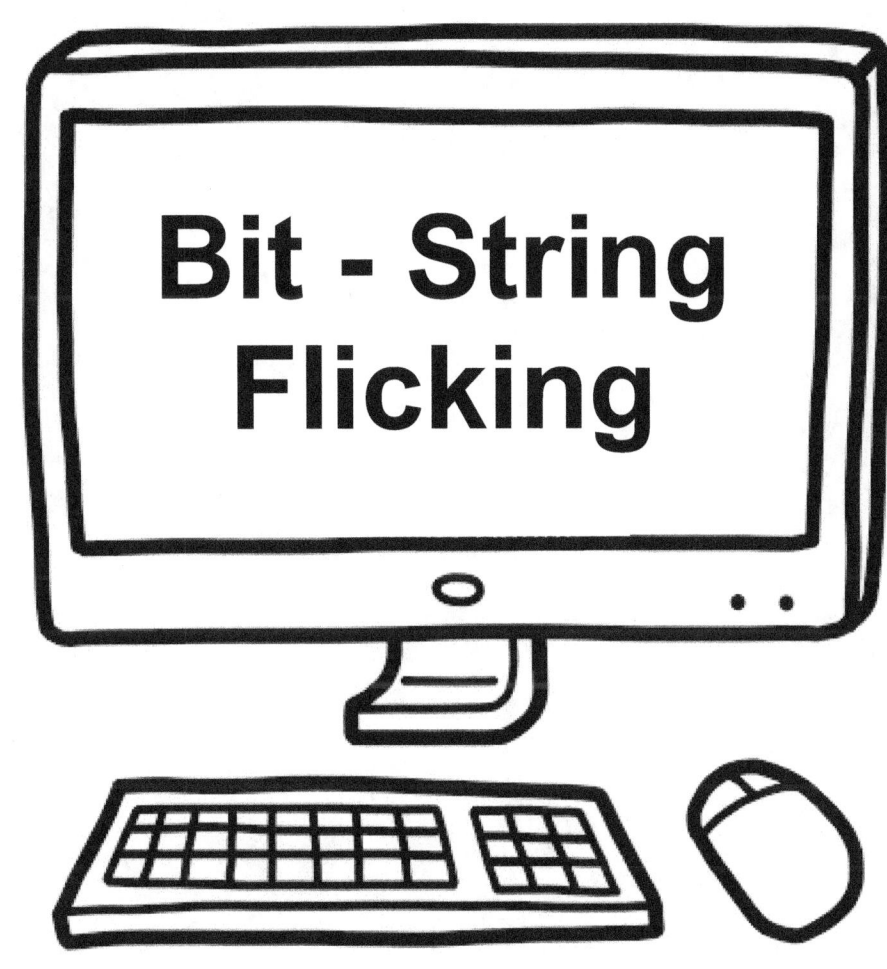

BIT STRING FLICKERING

As the name says, first let's learn about Bit and its details, then strings and Flickering

(I) Bitwise Operators

<u>The logical operators</u>:
    (1) Binary Operators: **and** (&), **or** (|), and **xor** ($\oplus$)
    (2) Unary Operator: **not** (~ or ¬)

BINARY OPERATORS:

- **or** is a logical binary operator of each bit in each of its operands.
  The **or** of two values is 1 only if one or both values are 1 else 0

<u>Example:</u>
    1010100 or 1100001 = 1110101

x	y	x or y
1	1	1
0	1	1
1	0	1
0	0	0
1	0	1
0	0	0
0	1	1

ACSL
Bit String Flicking

Sample

- **and** is a logical binary operator of each bit in each of its operands.
  The **and** of two values is 1 only if both values are 1 else 0.

Example:
  1010100 and 1100001 = 1000000

x	y	x or y
1	1	1
0	1	0
1	0	0
0	0	0
1	0	0
0	0	0
0	1	0

- **xor** is a logical binary operator of each bit in each of its operands.
  The **xor** of two values is 1 if the values are different or 0
  It is equal to zero if the value is equal to 1 in both x and y

Example:
  1010100 xor 1100001 = 011111

ACSL
Bit String Flicking

x	y	x xor y
1	1	0
0	1	1
1	0	1
0	0	1
1	0	1
0	0	1
0	1	0

UNARY OPERATORS:

- **not** is a logical unary operator that performs negation on each bit.   Bit 0 becomes 1 and vice.

Example:
not 1010100 = 0101011
not 1100001 = 0101011

x	y	not x	not y
1	1	0	0
0	1	1	1
1	0	0	0
0	0	1	1
1	0	0	0
0	0	1	1
0	1	1	1

(II) Strings

Logical shifts **LSHIFT-x** meaning "ripple" the bit-string x positions in the indicated direction, to the left. Bits shifted out are lost; zeros are shifted in at the other end. The size of a bit-string does not change with shift to left. If any bit strings are initially of different lengths, all shorter ones are padded with zeros in the left bits until all strings are of the same length

x	LSHIFT- x	LSHIFT-2 x	LSHIFT-3 x
001101	011010	110100	101000
101	010	100	000
11100	11000	10000	00000
11	10	00	000

Logical shifts **RSHIFT-x** meaning "ripple" the bit-string x positions in the indicated direction, to the right. Bits shifted out are lost; zeros are shifted in at the other end. The size of a bit-string does not change with shift to right. If any bit strings are initially of different lengths, all shorter ones are padded with zeros in the left bits until all strings are of the same length.

x	RSHIFT- x	RSHIFT-2 x	RSHIFT-3 x
001101	000110	000011	000001
101	010	001	000
11100	01110	00111	00011
11	01	00	00

Circulates LCIRC-x meaning "ripple" the bit string x positions in the indicated direction. As each bit is shifted out one end, it is shifted in at the other end. The effect of this is that the bits remain in the same order on the other side of the string.

The size of a bit-string does not circulate. If any bit strings are initially of different lengths, all shorter ones are padded with zeros in the left bits until all strings are of the same length.

x	LCIRC - x	LCIRC - 2 x	LCIRC - 3 x
001101	011010	110100	101001
101	011	110	101
11100	11001	10011	00111
11	11	11	11

Circulates **RCIRC-x** meaning "ripple" the bit string x positions in the indicated direction. As each bit is shifted out one end, it is shifted in at the other end. The effect of this is that the bits remain in the same order on the other side of the string.

The size of a bit-string does not circulate. If any bit strings are initially of different lengths, all shorter ones are padded with zeros in the left bits until all strings are of the same length.

x	RCIRC - x	RCIRC - 2 x	RCIRC - 3 x
001101	100110	010011	101001
101	110	011	101
11100	01110	00111	10011
11	11	11	11

(III) Flickering

The order of precedence

High to Low: NOT; SHIFT and CIRC; AND; XOR; and finally, OR.

"**Not**" is a Unary operator and it is evaluated first on a single operator with a precedence of right to left

As a thumb rule Operators are evaluated from right to left

Note: when a tie situation arises with equal precedence then ONLY, they are evaluated from left to right

ACSL
Bit String Flicking

Example Problems:

1. (RCIRC-2 1001010) AND (RSHIFT-1 1010011)
   = (1010010) AND (0101001)
   = 0000000

2. ((RSHIFT-2 (1010010 AND 1001010)) OR (LSHIFT-1 1011001))
   = ((RSHIFT-2 (1010010 AND 1001010)) OR 0110010)
   = ((RSHIFT-2 1000010) OR 0110010)
   = (0010000) OR 0110010
   = 0110010

ACSL
Bit String Flicking

Test 2

1. (RSHIFT-1 (LCIRC-2 (RCIRC-1 01110)))

2. (LSHIFT-2 (LSHIFT-2 (RCIRC-1 1111011)))

3. (LCIRC-1 (RCIRC-1 11110 OR LCIRC-2 11001))

4. (RCIRC-3 (LCIRC-1 111001 OR LSHIFT-2 100111))

5. (RCIRC-1 111001001 OR RSHIFT-2 100100111)

6. (LSHIFT-2 (LSHIFT-2 (RCIRC-1 11011))) OR LSHIFT-1 10001

ACSL
Bit String Flicking

Test 2

7. (LCIRC-3 (RCIRC-2 101011)) AND RSHIFT-1 100010

8. (RSHIFT-3 (LCIRC-2 (RCIRC-3 10111011)))

9. (LSHIFT-3 (LSHIFT-2 (RCIRC-4 000001111))) OR (LSHIFT-3 111110000)

10. (LCIRC-1 11001001 OR LSHIFT-2 10010011)

11. (LCIRC-1 (LCIRC-2 1011)) AND RSHIFT-1 1010

12. (LCIRC-3 (LCIRC-2 101010)) AND (LSHIFT-1 (RSHIFT-1 110010))

ACSL
Bit String Flicking

Test 2

13. (RCIRC-3 101111)) XOR RSHIFT-1 111010

14. (LSHIFT-2 (RSHIFT-2 (LCIRC-3 010001111))) XOR (LSHIFT-3 111110010)

ACSL
Bit String Flicking

15. (LSHIFT-3 (RCIRC-2 000001111)) XOR (LSHIFT-2 111110000)

16. NOT (LSHIFT-2 (LCIRC-2 000001111))

17. 1000111 XOR (LSHIFT-4 (RCIRC-2 0101011))

18. NOT (RSHIFT-3 (RCIRC-2 110001111))

19. (RCIRC-2 101011) OR (RSHIFT-1 111010)

20. NOT (LSHIFT-2 (RSHIFT-3 (RCIRC-3 001111)))

21. ((LCIRC-3 (10110 OR 11010)) AND (LSHIFT-1 10111))

22. (RCIRC-2 1001010) AND (RSHIFT-1 1010011)

23. ((RSHIFT-2 (1010010 AND 1001010)) OR (LSHIFT-1 1011001))

24. NOT ((00011 XOR 10101) AND 11100)

25. NOT ((0000011 XOR 1010001) OR 1001100)

26. LSHIFT-1 (NOT ((00011 XOR 10001) OR 10100))

27. (RSHIFT-2 (00000 XOR 10100)) AND (NOT 00011)

28. (RSHIFT-3 (1000010 XOR 1101000)) AND (RSHIFT-3 1011001)

29. (NOT (100011 OR 100111)) OR (100010 AND 100011)

30. (10010 OR 10011) AND (00000 AND (10000))

31. (LSHIFT-3 (RSHIFT-2 (LCIRC-1 11011))) OR LSHIFT-4 10001

32. (RCIRC-2 (LCIRC-3 101001)) AND RSHIFT-2 110010

33. (RSHIFT-2 (RCIRC-1 (LCIRC-2 100010))) XOR 100001

34. (LSHIFT-2 (LSHIFT-2 (RCIRC-2 001111))) OR (LSHIFT-2 (RCIRC-1 111000))

35. (LCIRC-1 110010 OR LSHIFT-2 100101) AND (NOT 111000)

36. (LCIRC-2 (LCIRC-1 10011)) AND (RSHIFT-2 (LCIRC-2 10100))

39. NOT (((LSHIFT-3 (RSHIFT-2 (LCIRC-2 010001111))) OR (LSHIFT-2 111110010))

40. (LSHIFT-2 (RCIRC-2 001001111)) OR (RSHIFT-2 110110000)

41. (NOT (RSHIFT-3 (LCIRC-2 000001111))) OR 100000001

42. 100011 XOR (LSHIFT-4 (RCIRC-2 010011))

43. (LCIRC-2 (LCIRC-2 1000011)) AND (RSHIFT-2 1000010)

44. (LCIRC-3 (LCIRC-3 101010)) XOR (LSHIFT-2 (RSHIFT-1 110010))

43. (LCIRC-2 (LCIRC-2 1000011)) AND (RSHIFT-2 1000010)

44. (LCIRC-3 (LCIRC-3 101010)) XOR (LSHIFT-2 (RSHIFT-1 110010))

45. ((RCIRC-3 100000 XOR RSHIFT-1 111010) OR (NOT (000001 AND 111110))

46. (LSHIFT-2 (RSHIFT-4 (LCIRC-3 0101111))) XOR (LSHIFT-2 1111110)

47. (RSHIFT-4 (LCIRC-2 000001111)) OR (RSHIFT-2 111110000)

48. (NOT (LSHIFT-2 (LCIRC-2 11110000))) OR (LSHIFT-1 10101010)

49. 1000101 OR (LSHIFT-4 (RCIRC-2 (LSHIFT-2 0101001)))

50. NOT (LSHIFT-3 (RCIRC-2 (LCIRC-4 110001111)))

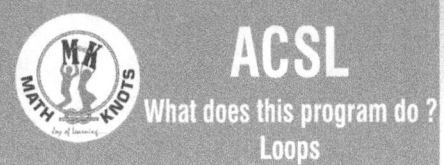

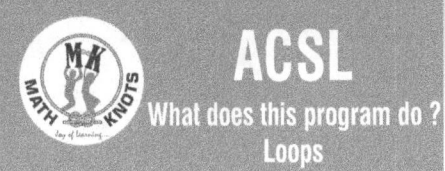

What does this program do ?

Students are given small code snippets to understand and analyze the programming concepts. The goal is to get them familiarize to understand and debug the software programs written in any language.

Four concepts are emphasized as below

- Looping
- Branching
- Arrays
- Strings

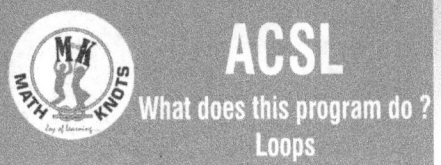

Test 2

1. What can the program do?
   ```
   for i = 1:1:5
      for j = 2:1:5
      k = i/j
      if k>2
         Output k
      end
      end
   end
   ```

2. What can the program do?
   ```
   k = 0
   for i = 1:1:6
      k = k+i
      if k>5
         PRINT k
      end
   end
   ```

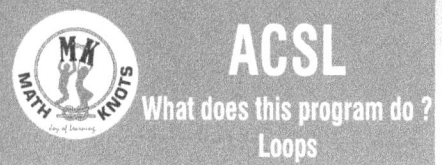

3. What will the output of the program?
   k = 0
   for i = 1:1:5
      k = k+i
      if k<5
         Output "small"
      else
         Output "big"
      end
   end

4. What is the output of the program?
   a = 2
   for i = 2:2:10
      a = a+$\frac{i}{2}$
      if a<(i+2)
         Output "*"
      elseif a>(i+2)
         Output "$"
      else
         Output "%"
      end
   end

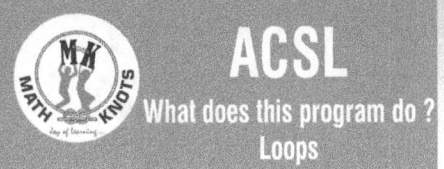

5. What is the output of the program?
   ```
   int rows, i, j, space;
   rows=4
   for (i=1; i<=rows;i++)
     for (j=1; j<=(2*i-1);j++)
       Output "$"
     Output "\n"
   ```

6. What is the output of the program?
   ```
   a = 2
   for i = 2:2:8
       a = a+i/2
       if a<(i/2)
          Output i
       elseif a>(i/2)
          Output i+1
       else
          Output 0
       end

   end
   ```

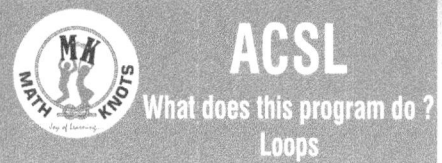

7. What is the output of the program?
   ```
   a = 1
   for i = 2:1:4
     j = 1
     a = a*i
     if a>(2*j)
         a=i
         Output i
   else
         Output 0
     end
   end
   ```

8. What is the output of the program?
   ```
   a = 2
   for i = 2:2:8
     %for j = 2:3
     j=1
   ```
   $a = a*\dfrac{i}{2}$
   ```
     if a>(2*j)
         a=i
         Output "*"
     else
         Output "-"
     end
   end
   ```

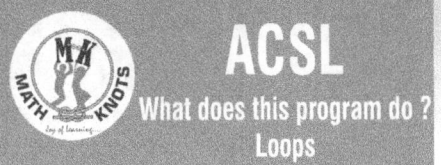

9. What is the output of the program?
   ```
   a = 2
   for i = 2:2:8
       j=i
       a = a*i/2
       if a>(2+j)
           Output j
       else
           Output i
       end
   end
   ```

10. What is the output of the program?
    ```
    a = 2
    for z = 2:2:8
        j=z
        a = a*z/2
        if a>(2+j)
            t = a
            PRINT t
        else
            PRINT "null"
        end
    
    end
    ```

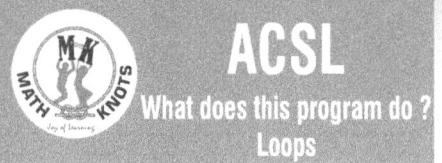

11. What is the output of the program?
    ```
    a = 2
    for z = 2:2:6
       a = a*z/2
       if a>(1+z)
          t = a
           Output t
       else
          Output "null"
       end

    end
    ```

12. What is the output of the program?
    ```
    o = 2
    for z = 2:6
       o = o*z/2
       if o>(1+z)
          t = o
        if t>20
           Output t
        end
       else
          Output "null"
       end
    end
    ```

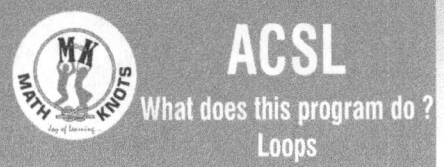

13. What is the output of the program?
    ```
    b = 1 ;
    for x = 1:2:5
        c = b/2
        a = x*c*2
        if a>18
            Output a
        else
            c = b/2
            Output c
        end
    end
    ```

14. What is the output of the program?
    ```
    for x = 2:6
        y=x+1
        if x < 5
        Output y
        end
    end
    ```

15. What is the output of the program?
    ```
    a = 't'
    for x = 2:2:10
       y = a
       if x>6
          Output "s"
       else
          Output a
       end
    
    end
    ```

16. What is the output of the program?
    ```
    for x = 2:2:4
       y = [ 1 0 ; 0 1]
       z = y*y
    end
    ```

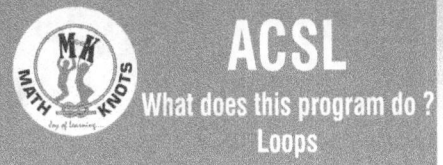

17. What is the output of the program?
```
c = 1
for x = 1:2:6
    b = x/2
    a = x*b*2
    if a>5
        Output a
    else
        c = x/2
        Output c
    end
end
```

18. What is the output of the program?
```
for x = 2:2:4
    y = [ 1 0 ; 0 1]
    z = y+y
end
```

19. What is the output?
    int i, x;
    int m =4
    for (i=m; i>=m; i - -)
    for (x=1; x<=1; j++)
    Output "|"
    Output "\n"

20. What is the output of the program?
    c = 1
    for x = 1:2:6
       b = x
       a = x*$\frac{b}{2}$
       if a>5
          Output a
       else
          c=$\frac{x}{2}$
          Output c
       end
    end

21. What is the output of the program?
```
c = 1
for x = 1:2:5
    b = c/2
    a = x*c*2
    if a>5
        Output a
    else
        c = b/2
        Output c
    end
end
```

22. What is the result after the entire loop?
```
for x = 1:2:5
    for y = 1:3
        z = x*y
        z = z+1
    end
end
```

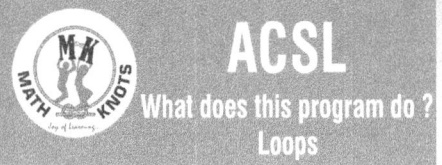

23. What is the value of a and b after the looping?
    ```
    for x = 1:2:5
        for y = 1:3
            if x<y || x == y
                a = x²+y²
            else
                b = x/y
            end
        end
    end
    ```

24. What is the value of a, b and c the program?
    ```
    for x = 1:2:5
        for y = 1:3
            if x<y
                a = x²
            elseif x>y
                b = y²
            else
                c = x/y
            end
        end
    end
    ```

25. What is the output of the program?
```
s = 0
for x = 1:4
    a = x
    b = x^a
    s = s+b
end
```

26. What is the output of every loop?
```
s = 0
for x = 1:4
    a = x
    b = x^a
    if x<2
    s = s+b
    elseif x>2
        s = s/b
    else
        s=0
    end
end
```

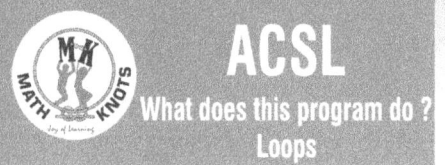

27. What is the program of the output?
```
for x = 1:7
   if x ==1
      Output "sunday"
   elseif x==2
      Output "monday"
   elseif x==3
      Output "tuesday"
   elseif x==5
      Output "thursday"
   elseif x==4
      Output "friday"
   elseif x==6
      Output "wednesday"
   else
      Output "saturday"
   end
end
```

28. What is the output of the program?
```
for x = 1:4
   x =x^x
end
```

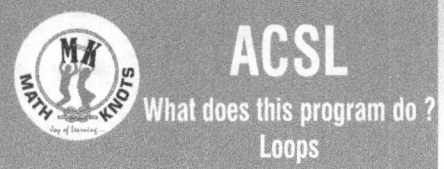

29. What is the output of the program?
    ```
    for x = 1:2:8
      if x>4
        x = x²
      elseif x<4
        x = 2*x
      else
        x = x/2
      end
    end
    ```

30. What is the output if rows=3?
    ```
    int i, j, space;
    int rows = 3;
    for (i=1; i<=rows;i++)
      for (j=1; j<=(2*i-1);j++)
        Output "*"
      Output "\n"
    ```

31. What is the output of the loop?
    for x = 2:2:8
      if x>4
        x = x^2
      elseif x<4
        x = 2*x
      else
        x = $\frac{x}{2}$
      end
    end

32. What is the output of the program?
    s = 0
    for x = 2:2:8
      for y = 1:3
        s = s+x
      end
    end

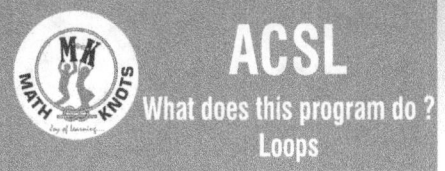

33. What is the value of *u* in the program?
    ```
    s = 2
    for x = 1:5
       s = s+x
       t = s*2
       u = t/s;
    end
    ```

34. What is the output of the program?
    ```
    s = 2
    a = 1
    b =
    for x = 1:5
      c = a*b
      c = c+2
    end
    ```

35. What is the output?
    int m, i, j;
    m=2
    for (i=m; i>=m; i--)
    for (j=1; j<=1; j++)
    Output "*"
    Output "\n"

36. What is the output of the program?
    sum = 0;
    for(c = 1; c <=5; ++c)
    sum += c ;
    Output sum

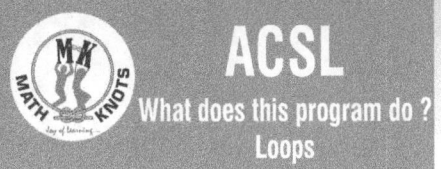

37. What is the output of the program?
    ```
    for x = 1:8
      if x<2
         Output "$\n"
      elseif x>2 && x<4
         Output "**\n"
      elseif x>4 && x<6
         Output "*$*\n"
      else
         Output "$$$\n"
    end
    end
    ```

38. What is the output of the program?
    ```
    sum = 0
    for(i = 1; i <= 10; i++)
    Output "%d * %d = %d \n", 5, i, 5*i)
    ```

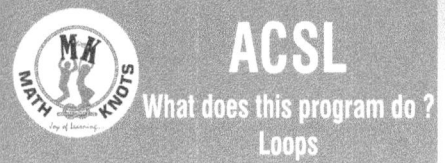

39. What is the output of the program?
    sum = 0
    n = 10
    for (i = 1; i <= 5; i++)
    Output "%d / %d = %d \n", n, i, n/I"

40. What is the output of the program?
    long long n
    int c = 0
    n = 5124
    while (n !=0)
    n/=10;
    ++c;
    Output c

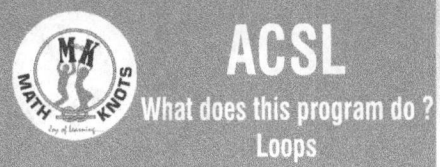

41. What is the output of the program?
    int number = 40
    if(number %2 == 0)
    Output "%d is even"
    else
    Output "%d is odd"

42. What is the output of the program rows = 5?
    int rows, i, j, space;
    rows=3
    for (i=1; i<=rows;i++)
    for (j=1; j<=(2*i-1);j++)
    Output "*"
    Output "\n"

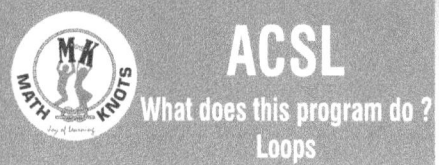

43. What is the value of q and r in the program?
    int n = 20, i = 3
    int quotient, remainder
    q = $\frac{n}{i}$
    r = n%i
    Output
    Output r

44. What is the output of the program?
    sum =
    n = 5
    for(i = 1; i <= n; i++)
    sum = sum+i
    Output sum

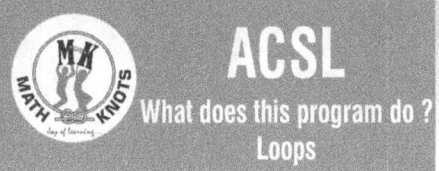

45. What is the output of the program after the loop is executed?
    sum = 0
    n = 10
    for(i = 1; i <= 5; i++)
    sum = $(sum * n + sum)^0$

46. What is the output of the program?
    s = 2
    a = 1
    b = 1
    for x = 1:5
      if x<3
        s=a^2+b^2
      elseif x>3
        s=$\frac{a}{b}$
      else
        s =0
    end
    end

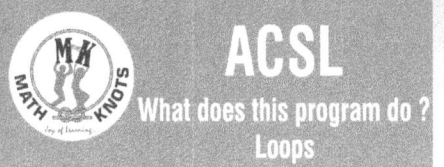

47. What is the output of the program?
    s = 2
    a = 1
    b = 1
    for x = 1:5
      if x<3
         s=$a^2+\frac{b}{2}$
      elseif x>3
         Output "termination"
         break
      else
         s =0
    end
    end

48. What is the output of the program?
    s = 5
    a = 1.5
    b = 2
    for x = 1:5
      if x<3
         s=$\frac{a}{2}+\frac{b}{2}$
      elseif x>3
         Output "termination"
         break
      else
           Output "-\n"
      end
      end

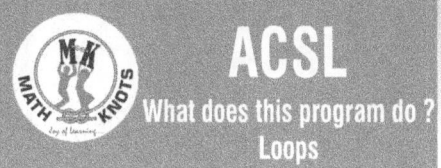

49. What is the output of the program?
    ```
    for x = 1:5
      if x<2
         Output "*\n"
      elseif x>2 && x<4
         Output "**\n"
      elseif x>4
         Output "***\n"
      else
         Output "$$$"

    end
    end
    ```

50. What is the output of the program if rows =4?
    ```
    int rows, i, j, space;
    rows=4
    for (i=1; i<=rows;i++)
    for (space = i; space<rows; space++)
    Output " "
    ```

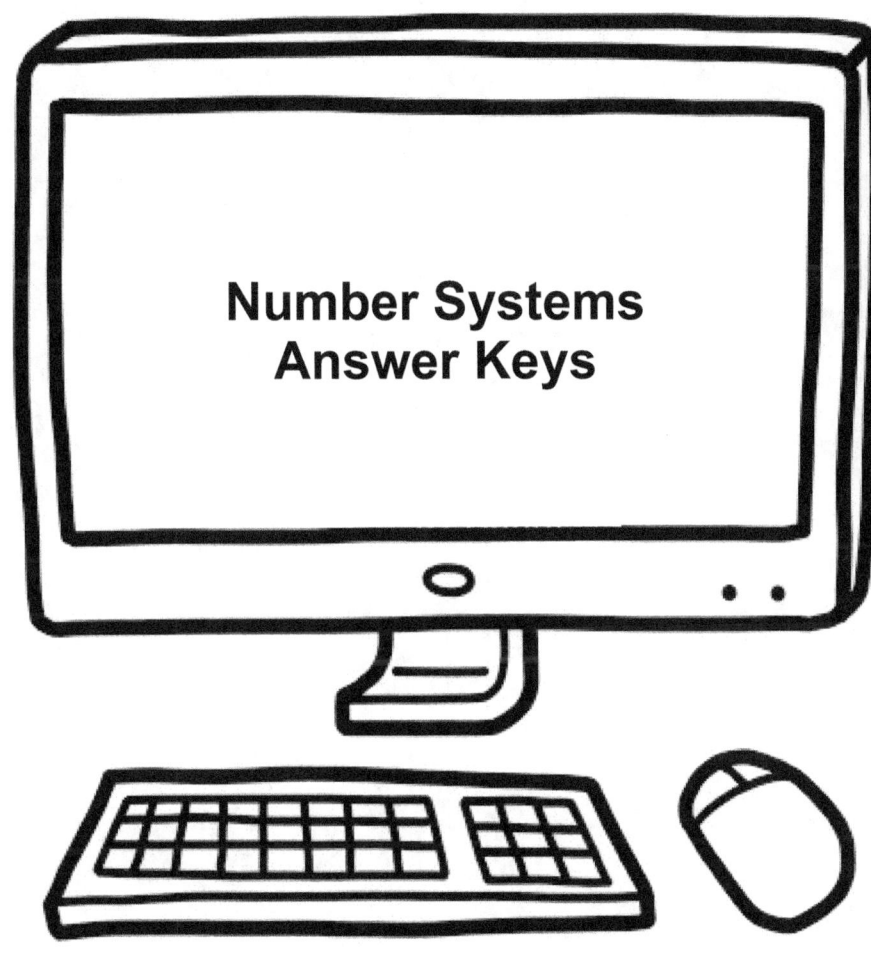

TEST 1

1. Convert the following to decimal system representation.
   100111

32	16	8	4	2	1
1	0	0	1	1	1

$= 1 \times 2^5 + 0 \times 2^4 + 0 \times 2^3 + 1 \times 2^2 + 1 \times 2^1 + 1 \times 2^0$
$= 32 + 4 + 2 + 1 = 39$

2. Convert the following to decimal system representation:
   101110

32	16	8	4	2	1
1	0	1	1	1	0

$= 32 + 8 + 4 + 2 = 46$

3. Convert the following to decimal system representation:
   1011111

64	32	16	8	4	2	1
1	0	1	1	1	1	1

$= 64 + 16 + 8 + 4 + 2 + 1 = 95$

4. Convert the following to decimal system representation:
   0011111

64	32	16	8	4	2	1
0	0	1	1	1	1	1

$= 16 + 8 + 4 + 2 + 1 = 31$

5. Convert the following to decimal system representation:
   1011010

64	32	16	8	4	2	1
1	0	1	1	0	1	0

$= 64 + 16 + 8 + 2 = 95$

ACSL
Computer Number Systems

TEST 1

6. Convert the following to binary system representation:
   30

128	64	32	16	8	4	2	1
30<128 so	30 < 64 so	30< 32 so	30 > 16 so 30–16=14	14 > 8 so 14-8=6	6> 4 so 6 -4 =2	2 = 2 so 2-2 = 0	0 < 1
0	0	0	1	1	1	1	0

00011110

7. Convert the following to binary system representation:
   45

128	64	32	16	8	4	2	1
45<128 so	45 < 64 so	45>32 45-32=13	13 < 16 so	13 > 8 so 13-8=5	5> 4 so 5 -4 =1	1 < 2 so	1= 1
0	0	1	0	1	1	0	1

00101101

8. Solve A - 50 = 10 and represent the answer in binary representation.
   A = 60

128	64	32	16	8	4	2	1
60<128 so	60 < 64 so	60> 32 60-32=28	28 > 16 so 28–16=12	12> 8 so 12-8=4	4= 4 so 4 -4 =0	0 < 2 so	0 < 1
0	0	1	1	1	1	0	0

00111100

11. Convert the following to decimal system representation:
    101100 + 101001

64	32	16	8	4	2	1
0	1 (check)	0	1 (check)	1 (check)	0	0

= 32 + 8 + 4 = 44

64	32	16	8	4	2	1
0	1	0	1	0	0	1

= 32 + 8 + 1 = 41
Therefore, 44 + 41 = 85

ACSL
Computer Number Systems

TEST 1

12. Solve A - 25 = 15 and represent the answer in binary representation.
    A = 40

128	64	32	16	8	4	2	1
40<128 so	40 < 64 so	40> 32 40-32=8	8 < 16 so	8= 8 so	0< 4 so	0 < 2 so	0 < 1
0	0	1	0	1	0	0	0

00101000

13. Convert the following to binary system representation:
    28

128	64	32	16	8	4	2	1
28<128 so	28<64 so	28 < 32	28 > 16 so 28-16=12	12> 8 so 12-8=4	4= 4 so 4-4 =0	0 < 2 so	0< 1
0	0	0	1	1	1	0	0

00011100

14. Solve A + 10 = 30 and represent the answer in binary representation.
    A = 20

128	64	32	16	8	4	2	1
20<128 so	20 < 64 so	20< 32 so	20 > 16 so 20–16=4	4 < 8 so	4= 4 so 4 -4 =0	0 < 2 so	0 < 1
0	0	0	1	0	1	0	0

00010100

15. Convert the following to decimal system representation:
    101001 - 000011

64	32	16	8	4	2	1
0	1 (check)	0	1 (check)	0	0	1 (check)

=32 + 8 + 1 = 41

64	32	16	8	4	2	1
0	0	0	0	0	1	1

= 2+1= 3

Therefore, 41 - 3 = 38

TEST 1

16. Convert the following to decimal system representation:
    11101 + 10001

64	32	16	8	4	2	1
0	0	1 (check)	1 (check)	1 (check)	0	1 (check)

=16 + 8 + 4 + 1 = 29

64	32	16	8	4	2	1
0	0	1 (check)	0	0	0	1 (check)

= 16+1 =17

Therefore, 29 + 17 = 46

17. Solve $x_8 = 1011$ $y_8 = 1000\ 0001$. Find $x_8 + y_8$
$$x_8 = 11 \quad y_8 = 129$$
$$x_8 + y_8 = 140$$

18. Convert the following to decimal system representation:
    111101 + 101010

64	32	16	8	4	2	1
0	1 (check)	1 (check)	1 (check)	1 (check)	0	1 (check)

=32 + 16 + 8 + 4 + 1 = 61

64	32	16	8	4	2	1
0	1	0	1	0	1	0

= 32 + 8 + 2= 42

Therefore, 61 + 42 = 103

19. Convert the following to decimal system representation:
    101101 + 001010

64	32	16	8	4	2	1
0	1 (check)	0	1 (check)	1 (check)	0	1 (check)

=32 + 8 + 4 + 1 = 45

64	32	16	8	4	2	1
0	0	0	1	0	1	0

= 8 + 2= 10

Therefore, 45 + 10 =55

TEST 1

20. Solve $A_8 = 0001\ 0001\ B_8 = 1100\ 0001.\ Find\ A_8 + B_8$
$$A_8 = 17\ B_8 = 193$$
$$A_8 + B_8 = 210$$

21. Convert the following to decimal system representation:
    101101 + 001011

64	32	16	8	4	2	1
0	1 (check)	0	1 (check)	1 (check)	0	1 (check)

=32 + 8 + 4 + 1 = 45

64	32	16	8	4	2	1
0	0	0	1	0	1	1

= 8 + 2+1= 11

Therefore, 45 + 11 =56

22. Convert the following to decimal system representation:
    1101001 - 0000111

64	32	16	8	4	2	1
1	1	0	1	0	0	1

=64+32+8+1 = 105

64	32	16	8	4	2	1
0	0	0	0	1	1	1

= 4+2+1=7

Therefore, 105 – 7 = 98

23. Convert 0xA6 to binary.
    A = 1010 which is 10 in decimal
    6 = 0110
    The binary representation will be 1010 0110

TEST 1

24. If $A_8 = 0010\ 0100\ \ B_8 = 1001\ 0000.$ Find $A_8 + B_8$
$$A_8 = 36\ \ B_8 = 128 + 16 = 144$$
$$A_8 + B_8 = 180$$

25. Convert 0XB 7 to binary.
    B = 1011
    7 = 0111
    The binary representation will be 1011 0111

26. Add 0xA4 and 0xC3 by converting into decimal.
    We know A = 10
    So 0Xa4 = (16 x 10) + (1 + 4) = 164

    And C = 12
    So 0xC3 = (16 x 12) + (3 x 1) = 195
    The sum = 359

27. Convert 232 into hexadecimal.

    ```
    16 | 232
    16 |  14    Reminder 8
       |   0    14
    ```

    =0xE8

28. Solve $A_8 = 1001\ 0001\ \ B_8 = 0100\ 0001.$ Find $A_8 - B_8$
$$A_8 = 145\ \ B_8 = 65$$
$$A_8 - B_8 = 80$$

29. Add 0xD8 and 0xA9 by converting into decimal.
    We know D = 13
    So 0xD8 = (16 x 13) + (1 + 8) = 216

    And A = 10
    So 0xA9 = (16 x 10) + (9 x 1) = 169
    The sum = 385

TEST 1

30. Convert 0xE2 to binary and then convert the binary to decimal.
    E = 1110
    2 = 0010
    The binary representation will be 1110 0010.
    = 128 +64+32+2 = 226

31. If $A_8 = 100\,001$ $B_8 = 0001\,1000$. Find $A_8 + B_8$
    $$A_8 = 129 \quad B_8 = 24$$
    $$A_8 + B_8 = 153$$

32. Convert the following to decimal system representation:
    010101 + 101011

32	16	8	4	2	1
0	1	0	1	0	1

    =16 + 4+ 1 = 21

32	16	8	4	2	1
1	0	1	0	1	1

    = 32 + 8 + 2 + 1 = 43
    Therefore, 21 + 43 = 64

33. Convert 167 into hexadecimal.

    ```
    16 | 167
    16 |  10    Reminder 7
       |   0       10
    ```

    Therefore, 7 = 0111 and 10 = A
    Ans: 0xA7

34. Solve $A_8 = 1000\,1001$ $B_8 = 0110\,0001$. Find $A_8 - B_8$
    $$A_8 = 137 \quad B_8 = 97$$
    $$A_8 - B_8 = 40$$

35. Solve 0XD4 - 0XAA by converting into decimal
    We know D = 13
    So 0xD4 = (16 x 13) + (1 x 4) = 212

    And A = 10
    So 0xAA = (16 x 10) + (1 x 10) = 170
    212-170 = 42

36. Convert 245 into hexadecimal.

    ```
    16 | 245
    16 |  15   Reminder 5
    16 |   1        1
       |   0        1
    ```

    = 0x511

37. Solve 0xAD2 – 0xA2B by converting into decimal.
    We know A = 10, D = 13
    So 0xAD4 = (256 x 10) + (16 x 13) + (1 x 2) = 2770

    And A = 10, B = 11
    So 0xAA = (256 x 10) + (16 x 2) + (1 x 11) = 2603
    2770 – 2603 = 167

38. Convert 250 into hexadecimal.

    ```
    16 | 250
    16 |  15   Reminder 10
    16 |   1        1
       |   0        1
    ```

    =0x11A

39. Solve 0xAC3 – 0xA2 by converting into decimal.
    We know A = 10, C = 12
    So 0xAC3 = (256 x 10) + (16 x 12) + (1 x 3) = 2755

    And A = 10
    So 0xA2 = (16 x 10) + (1 x 2) = 162
    2755 – 162 = 2593

40. Add 0xA9 and 0xE5 by converting into decimal.
    We know A = 10
    So 0xA9 = (16 x 10) + (1 x 9) = 169

    And E = 14
    So 0xE5 = (16 x 14) + (5 x 1) = 229
    The sum = 398

41. Convert 120 into hexadecimal.

    ```
    16 | 140
    16 |  8    Reminder 12
       |  0       8
    ```

    =0x8C

42. Solve $A_8 = 0001\ 1000\ 0001$ $B_8 = 1000\ 0001$. Find $A_8 - B_8$
    $$A_8 = 385\ \ B_8 = 129$$
    $$A_8 - B_8 = 256$$

43. Convert 340 into hexadecimal.

    ```
    16 | 340
    16 |  21   Reminder 4
    16 |   1      5
       |   0      1
    ```

    = 0x154

TEST 1

44. Convert 242 into hexadecimal.

```
16 | 242
16 |  15    Reminder 2
16 |   1        1
   |   0        1
```

= 0x112

45. Solve $A_8 = 0001\ 0001\ 0001$ $B_8 = 0101\ 0001$. Find $A_8 - B_8$

$$A_8 = 282 \quad B_8 = 81$$
$$A_8 - B_8 = 201$$

46. Convert the following to decimal system representation:
    100101 + 101000

32	16	8	4	2	1
1	0	0	1	0	1

=32 + 4 + 1 = 37

32	16	8	4	2	1
1	0	1	0	0	0

= 32 + 8 = 40

Therefore, 37 + 40 = 77

47. Convert 0xB7A to binary.

B = 1011
7 = 0111
A = 1010

The binary representation will be 1011 0111 1010

48. Convert 350 into hexadecimal.

```
16 | 350
16 |  21    Reminder 14
16 |   1        5
   |   0        1
```

= 0x15E

TEST 1

49. Convert the following to decimal system representation:
    101111 - 101000

32	16	8	4	2	1
1	0	1	1	1	1

=32 + 8 + 4 + 2 + 1 = 47

32	16	8	4	2	1
1	0	1	0	0	0

= 32 + 8 = 40

Therefore, 47 − 40 = 7

50. Solve $A_8 = 0001\ 0000\ 0011$ $B_8 = 0001\ 0000\ 0001$. Find $A_8 - B_8$
$$A_8 = 259 \quad B_8 = 257$$
$$A_8 - B_8 = 2$$

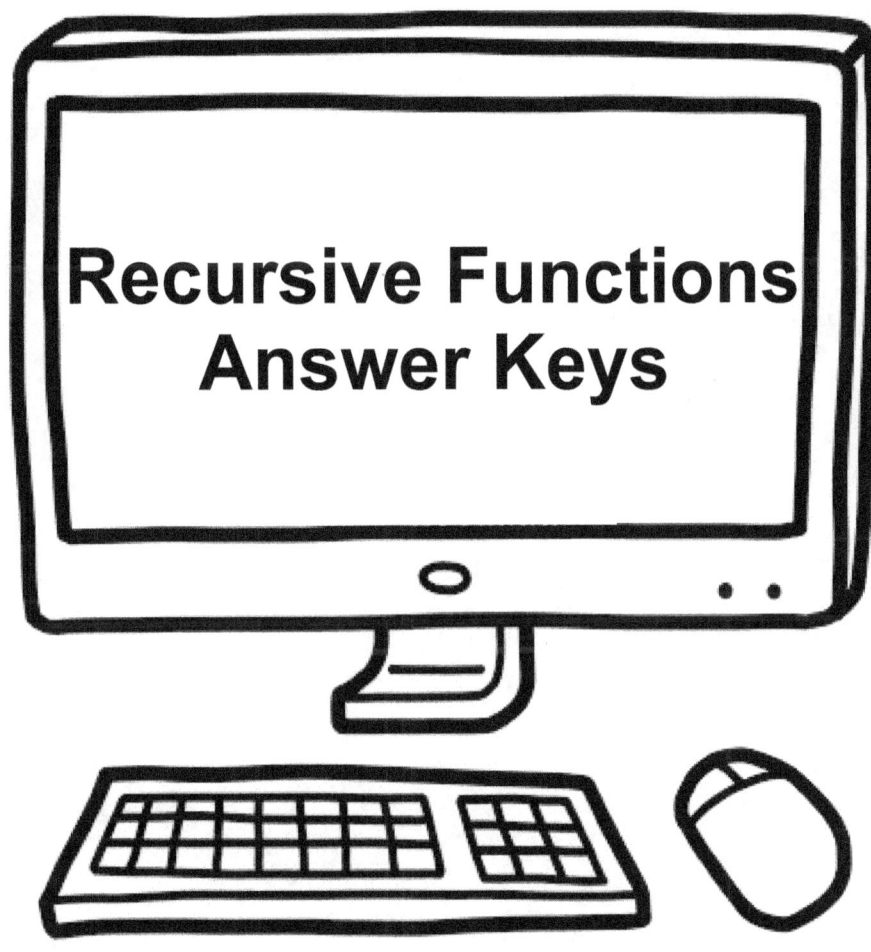

ACSL
Recursive functions

TEST 1

1. Evaluate the following recursive functions:
   Find $f(5,3)$

   $$f(x,y) = \begin{cases} f(x-1,y) & \text{when } x > y \\ x - y & \text{otherwise} \end{cases}$$

   $= f(4,3)$
   $= f(3,3) = 0$

2. Find $f(8,2)$

   $$f(x,y) = \begin{cases} f(x-2, y+1) & \text{when } x > y \\ x + y & \text{otherwise} \end{cases}$$

   $= f(6,3)$
   $= f(4,4) = 8$

3. Find $f(9,5)$

   $$f(x,y) = \begin{cases} f(x-y, y+1) & \text{when } x > y \\ x + y & \text{otherwise} \end{cases}$$

   $= f(4,6) = 10$

4. Find $f(20,5)$

   $$f(x,y) = \begin{cases} f(f(x-y, y+1)) & \text{when } x > y \\ x + y & \text{otherwise} \\ 1 & 0 \leq x \leq 10, y = non-existent \\ 0 & x > 10, y = non-existent \end{cases}$$

   $= f(f(15,6))$
   $= f(f(9,7))$
   $= f(f(2,8)) = f(2+8) = f(10) = 1$

5. Find $f(8,5)$

   $$f(x,y) = \begin{cases} f(f(x, y+1)) & \text{when } x > y \\ x + \dfrac{y}{x} & \text{otherwise} \\ 5 & 0 \leq x \leq 10, y = non-existent \\ 10 & x > 10, y = non-existent \end{cases}$$

   $= f(f(8,6))$
   $= f(f(8,7))$
   $= f(f(8,8)) = f(f(9)) = f(5) = 5$

TEST 1

6. Find $f(9,11)$

$$f(x,y) = \begin{cases} f(f(x, y-x)) & \text{when } x < y \\ x + \dfrac{x}{y} & \text{otherwise} \\ 0 & 0 \leq x \leq 5, y = non - existent \\ 1 & x > 5, y = non - existent \end{cases}$$

$= f(f(9,2))$
$= f(f(9,2)) = f(13.5) = 1$

7. Find $f(4,10)$

$$f(x,y) = \begin{cases} (f(x, y-x)) & \text{when } x < y \\ f(x-1, y+1) & \text{when } x > y \\ x + y & \text{otherwise} \end{cases}$$

$= (f(4, 10-4)) = (f(4,6))$
$= (f(4, 6-4)) = f(4,2)$
$= f(3,3) = 6$

8. Find $f(10,8)$

$$f(x,y) = \begin{cases} f(x-1, y+2) & \text{when } x > y \\ x + \dfrac{y}{x^{\frac{1}{2}}} & \text{otherwise} \end{cases}$$

$= f(9,10) = 9 + \dfrac{10}{3} = 12.33$

9. Find $f(5)$

$$f(x) = \begin{cases} f(x-2) + 2 & \text{when } x > 2 \\ 0 & x = 1 \\ 1 & x = 2 \end{cases}$$

$f(5) = f(3) + 2 = 4$
$f(3) = f(1) + 2 = 2$
$= f(1) = 0$

10. Find $f(5)$ if $f(x) = 3.f(x-2) + 3$ and we know that $f(1) = 10$

$f(1) = 10$: Given
$f(3) = 3.f(1) + 3 = 30 + 3 = 33$
$f(5) = 3.f(3) + 3 = 3(33) + 3 = 99 + 3 = 102$

11. Evaluate the following recursive functions:
Find $f(3)$

$$f(x) = \begin{cases} f(x-1) - 1 & \text{when } x > 1 \\ 0 & x = 1 \\ 1 & x = 0 \end{cases}$$

$f(0) = 1$
$f(1) = 0$
$f(2) = f(2-1) - 1 = f(1) - 1 = -1$
$f(3) = f(3-1) - 1 = f(2) - 1 = -2$

12. Find $f(4,2)$

$$f(x,y) = \begin{cases} f(x - \frac{3}{2}, y-1) & \text{when } x > y \\ x + \frac{y}{x^2} & \text{otherwise} \end{cases}$$

$= f(2.5, 1) = f(1, 0) = f(-0.5, -1)) = f(-2, -2) = -2 + (\frac{-2}{-2^2}) = -1.5$

13. Find $f(4,5)$

$$f(x,y) = \begin{cases} f(x+y, y-1^3) & \text{when } x < y \\ x + y & x = \text{even} \\ x - y & x = \text{odd} \end{cases}$$

$= f(9, 4) = 5$

14. Find $f(4,8)$

$$f(x,y) = \begin{cases} (f(x+1, y-2)) & \text{when } x < y \\ x + y & \text{otherwise} \end{cases}$$

$= f(5, 6) = f(6, 4) = 10$

ACSL
Recursive functions

TEST 1

15. Find $f(7,5)$

$$f(x,y) = \begin{cases} f(f(x-1, y+\frac{3}{2})) & \text{when } x > y \\ x - \frac{y}{x}, y & \text{otherwise} \end{cases}$$

Subject to conditions $f(x,y) = x + y$, for $y - x \geq 2.5$

Subject to conditions $f(x,y) = x + y$, for $y - x \geq 2.5$
$= f(f(6, 6.5))$
$= f(5.1, 6.5) = f(3.8, 6.5)$; According to question $= 3.8 + 6.5 = 10.3$

16. Find $f(9,4)$

$$f(x,y) = \begin{cases} f(f(x, y^2 - 4)) & \text{when } x > y \\ x + \frac{2x}{4y} & \text{otherwise} \\ 1 & x > 5 \text{ and } y \text{ is non} - \text{existent} \end{cases}$$

$= f(f(9,12))$
$= f(9.375) = 1$

17. Find $f(2,8)$

$$f(x,y) = \begin{cases} f(x+y, y-1) & \text{when } x < y \\ f(x-3, y) & \text{when } x > y \\ x + \frac{y}{x^2} & \text{otherwise} \end{cases}$$

$= f(10, 7) = f(7, 7) = \frac{50}{7}$

18. Find $f(a, b)$ where $a > b$ and $a - b = 1$

$$f(x,y) = \begin{cases} f(x-2, y+2) & \text{when } x > y \\ x + \frac{y}{x^{\frac{1}{2}}} & \text{otherwise} \end{cases}$$

$= f(a-2, b+2) = $ or $f(b-1, b+2)$
Therefore, $f(x,y) = a + \frac{b}{a^{\frac{1}{2}}}$

ACSL
Recursive functions

TEST 1

19. Find $f(a)$ where is the biggest even number ranging between 1 and 10

$$f(x) = \begin{cases} f(x-2) + 2 & \text{when } x > 2 \\ 0 & x = 1, 0 \\ 1 & x = 2 \end{cases}$$

$f(0) = 0$
$f(1) = 0$
$f(2) = 1$
$f(3) = f(1) + 2 = 2$
$f(4) = f(2) + 2 = 3$
$f(5) = f(3) + 2 = 5$
$f(6) = f(4) + 2 = 5$
$f(7) = f(5) + 2 = 7$
$f(8) = f(6) + 2 = 7 = f(a)$

20. Find $f\left(49^{\frac{1}{2}}\right)$

$$f(x) = \begin{cases} f(x-2) + x & \text{when } x > 2 \\ 0 & x = 1, 0 \\ 1 & x = 2 \end{cases}$$

$f(0) = 0$
$f(1) = 0$
$f(2) = 1$
$f(3) = f(1) + 3 = 3$
$f(4) = f(2) + 4 = 4$
$f(5) = f(3) + 5 = 8$
$f(6) = f(4) + 6 = 10$
$f(7) = f(5) + 7 = 15$

21. Evaluate the following recursive functions:

$$f(x) = \begin{cases} \text{Find } f(5) & \\ f(x-1) - \frac{1}{2} & \text{when } x > 1 \\ -1 & x = 1 \\ 1 & x = 0 \\ 0 & x = 2 \end{cases}$$

Write the complete series in the end.

$f(2) = 0$
$f(3) = f(2) - \frac{1}{2} = -0.5$
$f(4) = f(3) - \frac{1}{2} = -1$
$f(5) = f(4) - \frac{1}{2} = -1.5$

The complete series is : $1, -1, 0, -0.5, -1, -1.5$

22. Find $f(6,2)$

$$f(x,y) = \begin{cases} f(\frac{x}{y}, y) & \text{when } x > y \\ x + \frac{y}{x^2} & \text{otherwise} \end{cases}$$

$= f(3,2) = f(1.5,2) = 1.5 + \frac{2}{1.5^2} = 2.38$

23. Find $f(3,6)$

$$f(x,y) = \begin{cases} f(f(x+y,y)) & \text{when } x < y \\ x - y & \text{otherwise} \\ 0 & 1 \leq x \leq 10, y = non-existent \end{cases}$$

$= f(f(9,6)) = f(3) = 0$

24. Find $f(a,b)$ where $a > b$ and $a = b - a$

$$f(x,y) = \begin{cases} f(x, y+a) & \text{when } x < y \\ x + y & \text{otherwise} \end{cases}$$

$= f(a, b+a) = a + b + a = 2a + b$

25. Find $f(8,6)$

$$f(x,y) = \begin{cases} f(x-y, y) & \text{when } x > y \\ x - \frac{y}{x} & \text{otherwise} \end{cases}$$

$= f(2,6) = 2 - 3 = -1$

26. Find $f(5,4)$

$$f(x,y) = \begin{cases} f(f(x-1, y+4)) & \text{when } x > y \\ x + \frac{2x}{4y} & \text{otherwise} \\ 1 & x > 5 \text{ and } y \text{ is } non-existent \\ 0 & x < 5 \text{ and } y \text{ is } non-existent \end{cases}$$

$= f(f(4,8)) = f(4.25) = 0$

TEST 1

27. Find $f(1,6)$

$$(x,y) = \begin{cases} f(2x, y-1) & \text{when } x < y \\ f(x+3, \frac{y}{6}) & \text{when } x > y \\ x + \frac{y}{x^2} & \text{otherwise} \end{cases}$$

$= f(2,5) = f(4,4) = 4 + \frac{1}{4} = \frac{17}{4}$

28. Find $f(7,4)$

$$(x,y) = \begin{cases} f(x-2, y+2) & \text{when } x > y \\ x + y^2 & \text{otherwise} \end{cases}$$

$= f(5,6) = 5 + 36 = 41$

29. Find $f(5)$

$$(x,y) = \begin{cases} f(x-2) + x & \text{when } x > 1 \\ 0 & x = 1,0 \end{cases}$$

$f(1) = 0$
$f(3) = f(1) + 3 = 3$
$f(5) = f(3) + 5 = 8$

30. Find $f(4)$

$$f(x) = \begin{cases} f(x + x^2) & \text{when } x > 2 \\ 4 & x = 1,0 \\ -2 & x = 2 \end{cases}$$

$f(0) = 4$
$f(1) = 4$
$f(2) = -2$
$f(3) = 3 + 3^2 = 12$
$f(4) = 4 + 4^2 = 20$

TEST 1

31. Evaluate the following recursive functions:

$$a(x) = \begin{cases} \text{Find } a(4) \\ a(1) = -4 \\ a(n) = a(n-1) + 4 \end{cases}$$

$a(1) = -4$

$a(2) = a(1) + 4 = 0$

$a(3) = a(2) + 4 = 4$

$a(4) = a(3) + 4 = 8$

32. Find $a(5)$

$$a(x) = \begin{cases} a(0) = 2 \\ a(1) = 1 \\ a(n) = a(n-2) + n \end{cases}$$

$a(1) = 1$
$a(3) = a(1) + 3 = 4$
$a(5) = a(3) + 5 = 9$

33. Find $C(5)$

$$C(x) = \begin{cases} C(0) = a \\ C(1) = b \\ C(n) = C(n-1) + 2 \end{cases}$$

$C(1) = b$
$C(2) = b + 2$
$C(3) = b + 4$
$C(4) = b + 6$
$C(5) = b + 8$

ACSL
Recursive functions

TEST 1

34. Find $C(6)$

$$C(x) = \begin{cases} C(0) = \dfrac{a}{2} \\ C(1) = b \\ C(n) = C(n-2) + n \end{cases}$$

$C(0) = \dfrac{a}{2}$

$C(2) = \dfrac{a}{2} + 2 = \dfrac{a+4}{2}$

$C(4) = \dfrac{a+4}{2} + 4 = \dfrac{a+12}{2}$

$C(6) = \dfrac{a+12}{2} + 6 = \dfrac{a+24}{2}$

35. Find $f(4)$

$$f(x) = \begin{cases} f(f(x-1)) & x > 1 \\ 1 & x = 1 \end{cases}$$

$f(1) = 1$
$f(2) = f(f(1)) = f(1) = 1$
$f(3) = f(f(2)) = 1$
$f(4) = f(f(3)) = 1$

36. Find $f(4)$

$$f(x) = \begin{cases} f(x-1) + a & x > 1 \\ 0 & x = 1 \end{cases}$$

$f(1) = 0$
$f(2) = a$
$f(3) = 2a$
$f(4) = 3a$

TEST 1

37. Complete the missing values in the recursive formula of the sequence: 2, 8, 14, ...

$$\begin{cases} a(1) = A \\ a(n) = e(n-1) + B \\ A = ?, B = ? \end{cases}$$

The two parts of the formula should give the following information:
1. The first term (which is 2)
2. The rule to get any term from its previous term (which is 6)

Therefore, the recursive formula becomes:

$$\begin{cases} a(1) = 2 \\ a(n) = e(n-1) + 6 \end{cases}$$
$A = 2, B = 6$

38. Complete the missing values in the recursive formula of the sequence: -1, -4, -7, ...

$$\begin{cases} a(1) = A \\ a(n) = e(n-1) + B \\ A = ?, B = ? \end{cases}$$

The two parts of the formula should give the following information:
1. The first term (which is -1)
2. The rule to get any term from its previous term (which is -3)

Therefore, the recursive formula becomes:

$$\begin{cases} a(1) = -1 \\ a(n) = e(n-1) + (-3) \end{cases}$$
$A = -1, B = -3$

39. Find $f(5)$

$$f(n) = \begin{cases} f(n-2) + \dfrac{n}{2} & n > 3 \\ 1 & n = 1 \\ 0 & n = 0 \end{cases}$$

$f(1) = 1$
$f(3) = f(1) + \dfrac{3}{2} = 2.5$
$f(5) = f(3) + \dfrac{5}{2} = 5$

ACSL
Recursive functions

TEST 1

40. Find $f(a,b)$ where $a > b$ and $a = b - a$

$$f(x,y) = \begin{cases} f(\frac{x}{2}, \frac{y}{8} + \frac{a}{2}) & \text{when } x < y \\ x + \frac{y}{2} & \text{otherwise} \end{cases}$$

$= f(a, b+a) = a + \frac{b}{2} = a + \frac{2a}{2} = 2a$

41. Evaluate the following recursive function:

Find $f(8,6)$

$$f(x,y) = \begin{cases} f(x-1, y) & \text{when } x > y \\ x - \sqrt{y} & \text{otherwise} \end{cases}$$

$= f(7,6) = f(6,6) = 6 - \sqrt{6}$

42. Find $f(6,3)$

$$f(x,y) = \begin{cases} f(x-1, y+1) & \text{when } x > y \\ x + (\frac{2x}{4y})^{\frac{1}{2}} & \text{otherwise} \end{cases}$$

$= f(5,4) = f(4,5) = 4 + (\frac{8}{20})^{\frac{1}{2}} = 4.63$

TEST 1

43. Find $f(3,6)$

$$(x,y) = \begin{cases} f(3x,y) & \text{when } x < y \\ f(x,y+3) & \text{when } x > y \\ x + \dfrac{yx}{x^{\frac{1}{2}}} & \text{otherwise} \end{cases}$$

$= f(3(3),6) = f(9,6)$

$= f(9,6+3) = f(9,9)$

$= 9 + \dfrac{81}{9^{\frac{1}{2}}} = 9 + \dfrac{81}{3} = 36$

44. Find $f(4)$

$$f(x) = \begin{cases} f(x-1) - (x^2) & \text{when } x > 1 \\ 1 & x = 1 \\ -2 & x = 0 \\ 0 & x = 2 \end{cases}$$

$f(2) = 0$
$f(3) = f(2) - (3^2) = -9$
$f(4) = f(3) - (4^2) = -25$

45. Find $f(12,3)$

$$f(x,y) = \begin{cases} f(\dfrac{x}{3}, y) & \text{when } x > y \\ f(x+1.7, y) & x < y \\ x + yx & x = y \end{cases}$$

$= f(4,3) = f(\dfrac{4}{3}, 3) = f(1.3, 3)$

$= f(3,3) = 3 + 9 = 12$

46. Find $f(2,4)$

$$f(x,y) = \begin{cases} f(x+y, \dfrac{y}{x}) & \text{when } x < y \\ f(x, y+4) & x > y \\ x + \dfrac{y}{x} + xy & x = y \end{cases}$$

$= f(2+4, \dfrac{4}{2}) = f(6,2)$

$= f(6, 2+4) = f(6,6)$

$= 6 + 1 + 36 = 43$

47. Find $f(3)$

$$f(x) = \begin{cases} f(1) = 1 \\ f(x) = f(x-1) + \dfrac{1}{x} \end{cases}$$

$f(1) = 1$

$f(2) = f(1) + \dfrac{1}{2} = 1.5$

$f(3) = f(2) + \dfrac{1}{3} = 1.5 + 0.33 = 1.83$

48. Find $a(4)$

$$a(n) = \begin{cases} a(0) = -2 \\ a(1) = -3 \\ a(n) = a(n-2) + n^2 \end{cases}$$

$a(0) = -2$
$a(2) = a(0) + 2^2 = 2$
$a(4) = a(2) + 4^2 = 18$

49. Find $a(5)$

$$a(x) = \begin{cases} a = 0 & \text{at } x = 0 \\ a = 1 & \text{at } x = 1 \\ a(x) = a(x-2) + \dfrac{x+1}{2} & \text{at other values of } x \end{cases}$$

$a(1) = 1$

$a(3) = a(1) + \dfrac{4}{2} = 3$

$a(5) = a(3) + \dfrac{6}{2} = 9$

50. Evaluate the following recursive functions:

$$f(x,y) = \begin{cases} \text{Find } f(6,3) \\ f\left(x - \dfrac{1}{2}, y\right) & \text{when } x > y \\ x - \dfrac{y}{xy} & \text{otherwise} \end{cases}$$

$= f\left(6 - \dfrac{1}{2}, 3\right)$
$= f(5.5, 3) = f(5 - 0.5, 3) = f(5, 3)$
$= f(4.5, 3)$
$= f(4, 3) = f(3.5, 3)$
$= f(3, 3) = 3 - \dfrac{3}{9} = 3 - \dfrac{1}{3} = \dfrac{8}{3}$

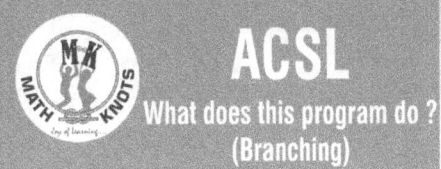
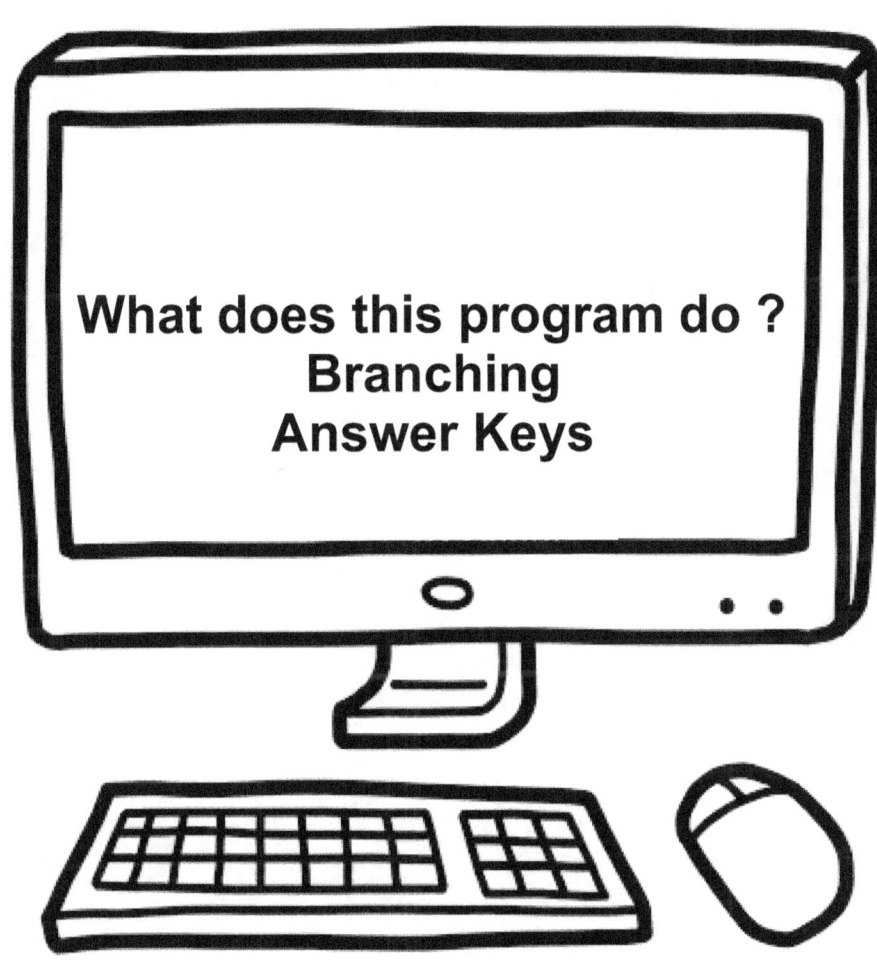

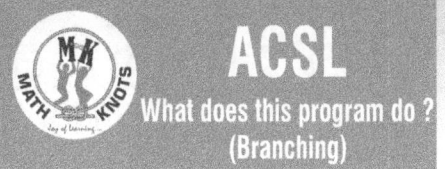

ACSL
What does this program do? (Branching)

Test 1

1. What is the output of the program?
b=-1;
if(b<0)
Output "The value is negative"
else Output "The value is positive"

Output:
The value is negative

2. What is the output of the program?
b= 0
if(b<0)
Output "The value is negative"
elseif (b>0)
Output "The value is positive"
else
Output "The value is the smallest whole number"

Output:
The value is the smallest whole number

3. What is the output of the program?
a= 5
b=5
if (a==b)
Output "True"

Output:
True

4. What is the output of the program if you enter A?
A=3
B=5
if (A==B)
Output "True"
else
Output "False"

Output:
False

5. What is the output of the program?
```
c = 0
while c< 8
output (c)
if c==4
break
c+=1
```

Output
0
1
2
3

6. What is the output of the program?
```
A = 0
for B = 7 to 21 step 7
A = A + B
next B
end
```

Output
42

7. What is the output of the program?
```
a=2
b=4
c = 0
d = 3
if a<b
   c=a+b
   d = c+b
   Output d
end
```

Output
10

ACSL
What does this program do?
(Branching)

Test 1

8. What is the output of the program?
a=8
b=4
c = 0
d = 0
if a>b
   c=a-b
   d = c+a
   Output d
end

Output
12

9. What is the output of the program?
a=5
b=3
c = 0
d = 0
if a>b
   c=a+b
   d = c+a
   Output d
end

Output
13

10. What is the output of the program?
a=5
b=3
c =0
d =0
e=0
f=0
if a>b
   c=a+b
   d = c+a
   e=b+c
   f=d+e
end
Output f

Output
24

ACSL
What does this program do?
(Branching)

Test 1

11. What is the output of the program?
```
a=5
b=3
c =0
d =0
e=0
f=0
if a>b && b>c
    c=a+b
    d = c-a
    e=b+c
    f=d+e
end
Output f
```

Output
14

12. What is the output of the program?
```
a=5
 for i= 1:10
   c=a+i
   if c>11
      break
   end
   Output c

end
```

Output
6
7
8
9
10
11

13. What is the output of the program?
```
a=4
for i= 1:2:12
   c=a+i
   if c>12
      break
   end
Output c

end
```
Output
5
7
9
11

14. What is the output of the program?
```
a=4
b=2
for i= 1:2:12
   c=a+i
   d=c+b
   if c>11
      break
   end
   Output d

end
```

Output
7
9
11

15. What is the output of the program?
```
a=3
b=3
for i= 1:2:12
   c=a+i
   d=c+b
   e=d+d
  Output e
end
```
Output
14
18
22
26
30

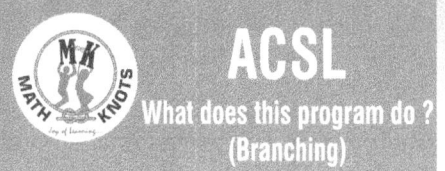

ACSL
What does this program do?
(Branching)

Test 1

16. What is the final output of the program?
a=2
b=3
for i= 1:2:12
  c=a+i
  d=c+b
  e=d+d
  Output e
end

Output
32

17. What is the output of the program?
a=2
b=3
for i= 1:2:12
  c=b+i
  d=c+b
  e=d+b
  Output e
end

Output
10, 12, 14, 16, 18, 20

18. What is the output of the program?
a=5
b=3
c = 0
d = 0
if a>b
  c=a+b
  a=10
  d = c+a
  Output d
else
Output "1"
end

Output
18

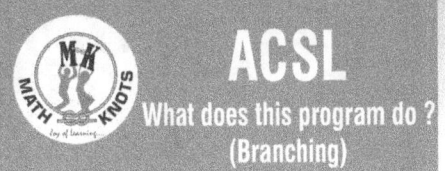

Test 1

19. What is the value of "g"?
```
a=5
b=3
c = 0
d = 0
if a>b
   c=a+b
   a=10
   d = c+a
 else
break
end
f=12
g=d+f
Output g
```

Output
30

20. What is the value of "g"?
```
a=2
b=3
c = 0
d = 0
if a<b
   c=a+b
   a=10
   d = c+a
 else
break;
end
f=10
g=d+f
Output g
```

Output
25

21. What is the output?
```
a=2
b=3
c = 0
d = 0
if a<b
   c=a+b
   a=c
   d = c+a

end
f=10
g=d+f
```

Output
g=20

22. What is the output of the program if the user enters 10?
```
t = 50
s=10
if t>s
   Output "smaller"
elseif Output "larger"
else
   Output "error"
end
```

Output
smaller

23. What is the value of a after the execution of the statement if a = 10 and b = 20?
a= (a <b) ? b : -b

Output
20

The above statement can be interpreted as:

```
if ( a < b )
{
   a = b;
}
else {
   a = -b;
}
```

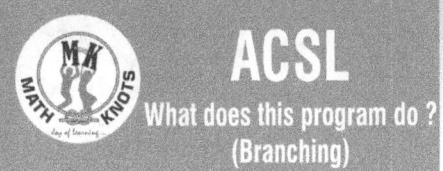

Test 1

24. What is the value of a after the execution of the statement if a = 45 and b = 35?
a= (a <b) ? b : -b

Output
-35

25. What is the output of the program if n = 10?
n= 10
if(n%2 == 0)
Output "even"
else
Output "odd"

Output
even

26. What is the output of the program if n = 19?
n= 19
if(n%2 == 0)
Output "even"
else
Output "odd"

Output
odd.

27.   What is the output of the statement if n = 144?
(n % 2 ==0) ? Output << n << "is even" : Output<< n << "is odd";

Output
144 is even

28. What is the output of the program?
n=8
i = true;
for (i=2; i<=n, ++i)
if (n% i==0)
iprime=false
Output "No"
break;
else
Output "Yes"

Output
No

29. What is the output of the program if n = 10?
```
n = 10
for(i=1; i<=n; ++i)
if(n%i==0)
Output i
```

Output
1 2 5 10

30. What is the output of the program?
```
int n=45, i;
 bool i = true;
for (i=2; i<=n, ++i)
 If (n % i==0)
 i = false;
 Output "No"
 break;
else
Output "Yes"
```

Output
Yes

31. What is the output of the statement?
```
int n=40
if(n%2 == 0)
Output "Yes"
else
Output "No"
```

Output
Yes

32. What is the output of the statement?
```
int n = 31;
(n%2==0) ? Output<< n << " Yes" : Output << n << "No";
```

Output
No

33. What is the output of the program?
```
int n = 10
int add(int n)
if (n!=0)
return n + add(n-1)
```

Output
55

Test 1

34. What is the output of the program?
```
int n=40
if(n/2 == 0)
Output "Yes"
else
Output "No"
```

Output
No

35. What is the output of the program if n = 10 and m = 12?
```
int n=10, m=12
if (n>m)
Output "n is larger"
else
Output "m is larger"
```

Output
m is larger

36. What is the output of the program?

```
t = 50 ;
s = 50
if t>s
   Output "smaller"
elseif t<s
Output "larger"
else
   Output "error"
end
```

Output
error

37. What is the output of the program if n= 12, m = 1, a = 15?
```
int n, m, a;
if (n>m && n>a)
{
Output "n"
elseif (m>n && m>a)
Output "m"
else
Output "a"
```

Output
a

38. What is the output of the program?
int n = 3995;
(n%2==0) ? Output << n << " Yes" : Output << n << "No";
Output
No

39. What is the output of the program n=1, m = 2, a =2?
int n, m, a
if (n>m && n>a)
{
Output "n"
elseif (m>n && m>a)
Output "m"
else
Output "a"

Output
a

40. What is the output of the program a=2, c=-2?
a= (a <c) ? -c : c ;

Output
-2

41. What is the output of the program?
int n = 6
Output (factorial(n))
int factorial (int n)
  if(n > 1)
     return n * factorial(n - 1);
  else
     return 1;

Output
720

42. What is the output of the program?
```
score = 90
if (score == 100)
grade = 'A';
Output "A"
else if (score >= 90)
grade = 'A'
Output "Excellent"
else if (score >= 80)
grade = 'B'
Output "B"
else if (score >= 70)
grade = 'C'
Output "Good"
else if (score >= 60)
grade = 'D'
else
grade = 'F'
```

Output
Excellent

43. What is the output of the program?
```
age = 20, height = 170
if(height == age)
   Output "Equal !"
else if(height < age)
   Output "Height!"
else if(height > age)
   Output "Age!"
```

Output
Age

44. What is the output of the program?
```
int age =40
if(age >= 35 && age <= 80)
    Output "You're between 35 and 80 and cannot save money on your health insurance!"
else
    Output "Contact the office, we may have deals for you"
```

Output
You're between 35 and 80 and cannot save money on your health insurance!

45. What is the output of the program if age=45?
```
int age;
output "Enter your age: "
if (age < 0 || age > 200)
   Output "Error."
else
   Output "Age entered"
```

Output
Age entered

46. What is the output of the program if x=8?
```
if (x > 0)
 Output "positive"
else if (x < 0)
 Output "negative"
else
 Output "zero"
```

Output
positive

47. What is the output of the program?
```
int num=9;
if(num == 1)
   Output "The number is 1"
else if(num == 2)
   Output "The number is 2"
else
   Output "The number is not 1 or 2"
```

Output
The number is not 1 or 2

48. What is the output of the program?
```
int a = 100;
if( a == 20 )
   Output "a is 20"
else if( a == 40 )
   Output "a is 40"
else if( a == 60 )
   Output "a is 60"
else
   Output "a does not match"
Output a
```

Output
a does not match
100

ACSL
What does this program do?
(Branching)

Test 1

49. What is the output of the program?
```
   int a = 20;
  if( a == 20 )
     Output "a is 20"
else if( a == 40 )
     Output "a is 40"
else if( a == 60 )
     Output "a is 60"
else
     Output "a does not match"
   Output a
```

Output
a is 20

50. What is the output of the program if n1=2 and n2=5?
```
   n1=2 and n2=5
   m = (n1 > n2) ? n1 : n2;
   do
      if (m % n1 == 0 && m % n2 == 0)
        Output m
        break;
     else
        ++m;
   while (true);
```

Output
10

ACSL
Pre/Post/In - fix Notation

Test 2

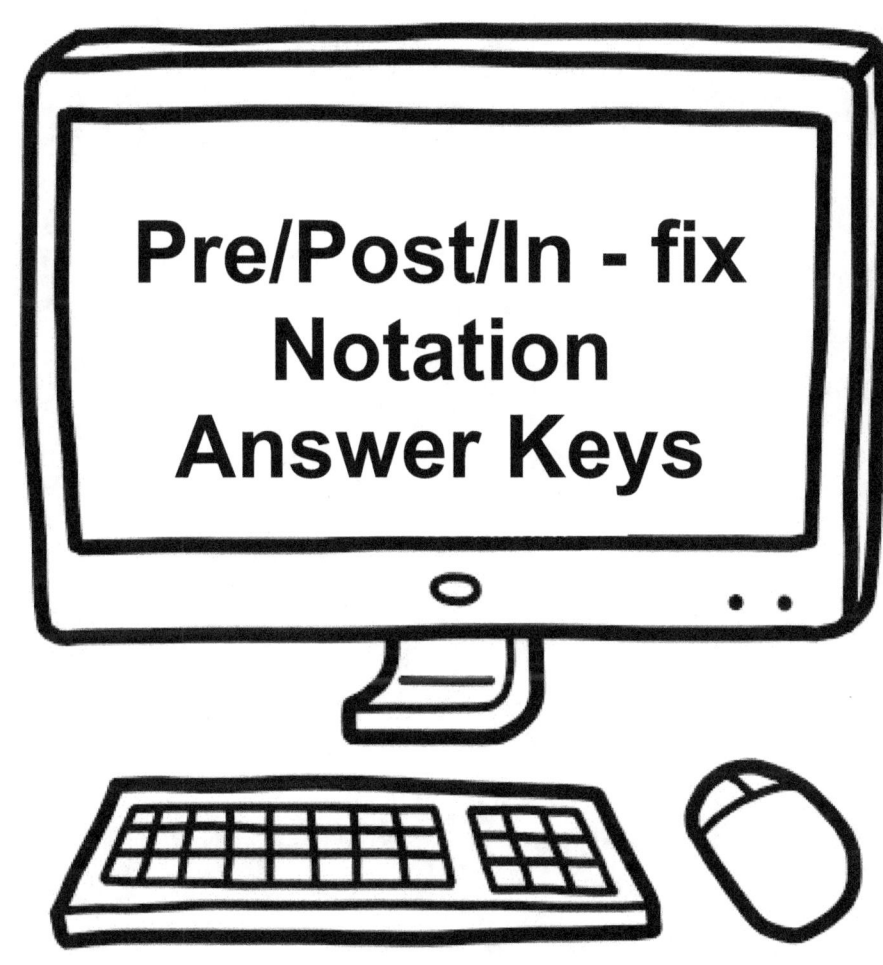

ACSL
Pre/Post/In-fix Notation

Test 2

1. Convert the following infix into prefix notations
$$A * \frac{B}{C} + D$$

$= (A * (\frac{B}{C})) + D$
$= (A * (/BC)) + D$
$= (*A/BC) + D$
$= + *A/BCD$

2. Convert the following infix to prefix notation:
$$A + B * C + D^E + E^D$$

$= ((A + (B*C)) + D^E) + E^D$
$= ((A + (*BC)) + D^E) + E^D$
$= ((+A*BC) + D^E) + E^D$
$= ++A*BC \uparrow DE + E^D$
$= +++A*BC \uparrow DE \uparrow ED$

3. Convert the following infix to prefix notation:
$$(A*B) + (C*\frac{A}{B})$$

$= (A*B) + (C * (\frac{A}{B}))$
$= (*AB) + (C * (/AB))$
$= (*AB) + (*C/AB)$
$= +*AB*C/AB$

4. Convert the following infix into postfix notations:
$$\frac{A + B + A^2 + B^2}{3}$$

$= \frac{(((A+B) + A^2) + B^2)}{3}$
$= \frac{(((AB+) + A^2) + B^2)}{3}$
$= \frac{((AB + A2\uparrow +) + B^2)}{3}$
$= \frac{(AB + A2\uparrow + B2\uparrow +)}{3}$
$= AB + A2\uparrow + B2\uparrow + 3/$

ACSL
Pre/Post/In - fix Notation

Test 2

5. Convert the following infix into postfix notation:
$$A * B * (C - B) * (D - A)$$
$= ((A * B) * (C - B)) * (D - A)$
$= ((AB *) * (CB -)) * (D - A)$
$= (AB * CB -*) * (DA-)$
$= AB * CB -* DA -*$

6. Convert the following prefix into infix notation
$$- * + ABB \uparrow C2$$
$= A + B * B - C \uparrow 2$
$= (A + B) * B - C^2$

7. Convert the following infix into prefix notation:
$$\frac{A-B}{C-D} + \frac{A^B}{C^D}$$
$= (\frac{(A-B)}{(C-D)}) + (\frac{A^B}{C^D})$
$= (\frac{(-AB)}{(-CD)}) + (\frac{A^B}{C^D})$
$= (/-AB - CD) + (\frac{\uparrow AB}{\uparrow CD})$
$= (/-AB - CD) + (/\uparrow AB \uparrow CD)$
$= +/-AB - CD/\uparrow AB \uparrow CD$

8. Convert the following infix to postfix notation:
$$A * B + C * A - B$$
$= ((A * B) + (C * A)) - B$
$= ((AB *) + (CA *)) - B$
$= (AB * CA * +) - B$
$= AB * CA * + B -$

9. Convert the following infix to postfix notation:
$$(\frac{D}{C} + \frac{C}{B} + \frac{B}{A})^E$$
$= (((\frac{D}{C}) + (\frac{C}{B})) + (\frac{B}{A}))^E$
$= (((DC/) + (CB/)) + (\frac{B}{A}))^E$
$= ((DC/CB/+) + (\frac{B}{A}))^E$
$= ((DC/CB/+) + (BA/))^E$
$= (DC/CB/+BA/+)^E$
$= DC/CB/+BA/+E \uparrow$

10. Convert the following infix to prefix notations:
$$(A - B) + \frac{C - D}{B}$$

$= (A - B) + (\frac{(C - D)}{B})$

$= (A - B) + (\frac{(-CD)}{B})$

$= (-AB) + (/-CDB)$

$= + - AB/-CDB$

11. Convert the following infix to prefix notation:
$$A * B + (A + B) + A^B$$

$= ((A * B) + (A + B)) + A^B$

$= ((* AB) + (+AB)) + A^B$

$= (+ * AB + AB) + A^B$

$= (+ * AB + AB) + (\uparrow AB)$

$= + +* AB + AB \uparrow AB$

12. Convert the following infix to postfix notation:
$$A * D * E * (A - C)$$

$= ((A * D) * E) * (A - C)$

$= (AD * E *) * (AC-)$

$= AD * E * AC -*$

13. Convert the following infix to postfix notations:
$$\frac{(A - \frac{B}{C})}{B - C}$$

$= \dfrac{(A - (\frac{B}{C}))}{(B - C)}$

$= \dfrac{(A - (BC/))}{(B - C)}$

$= \dfrac{(ABC/-)}{(BC-)}$

$= ABC/-BC -/$

Test 2

14. Convert the following infix to prefix notation:
$$(A - D) * (D - A) + \frac{B}{C}$$

$= ((A - D) * (D - A)) + (\frac{B}{C})$

$= ((-AD) * (D - A)) + (\frac{B}{C})$

$= ((-AD) * (-DA)) + (\frac{B}{C})$

$= (* -AD - DA) + (/BC)$

$= + * -AD - DA/BC$

15. Convert the following infix to postfix notation:
$$(A^2 + B^3 + (A - B)^4)$$

$= ((A^2 + B^3) + (AB-)^4)$

$= ((A^2 + B^3) + (AB - 4\uparrow))$

$= (((A2\uparrow) + (B3\uparrow)) + (AB - 4\uparrow))$

$= (((A2\uparrow)(B3\uparrow)+) + (AB - 4\uparrow))$

$= A2\uparrow B3\uparrow +AB - 4\uparrow +$

16. Convert the following prefix into infix notation:
$$+ - AB * \frac{C}{DA}, \text{where } A = B = 2, C = D = 3$$

$= + - AB (C * \frac{D}{A})$

$= +(A - B)(C * \frac{D}{A})$

$= (A - B) + (C * \frac{D}{A})$

$= (2 - 2) + (3 * \frac{3}{2}) = \frac{9}{2}$

17. Convert the following infix to prefix notation:
$$\frac{A - B}{C} + \frac{C}{A - B}$$

$= (\frac{(A - B)}{C}) + (\frac{C}{(A - B)})$

$= (\frac{(-AB)}{C}) + (\frac{C}{(A - B)})$

$= (/-ABC) + (\frac{C}{(A - B)})$

$= (/-ABC) + (\frac{C}{(-AB)})$

$= (/-ABC) + (/C - AB)$

$= +/-ABC/C - AB$

ACSL Pre/Post/In - fix Notation

Test 2

18. Convert the following infix notations into prefix notation:

$$A^{A^A} + \frac{\frac{B}{B}}{B}$$

$= (A^{A^A}) + (\frac{\frac{B}{B}}{B})$

$= (\uparrow A^A A) + (\frac{\frac{B}{B}}{B})$

$= (\uparrow\uparrow AAA) + ((/BB)/B)$
$= (\uparrow\uparrow AAA) + (//BBB)$
$= +\uparrow\uparrow AAA//BBB$

19. Convert the following infix notations into prefix notation:

$$A - B^3 + \frac{C}{D^2}$$

$= (A - B^3) + (\frac{C}{D^2})$

$= (A - (\uparrow B3)) + (\frac{C}{D^2})$

$= (-A \uparrow B3) + (\frac{C}{D^2})$

$= (-A \uparrow B3) + (\frac{C}{\uparrow D2})$

$= (-A \uparrow B3) + (/C \uparrow D2)$
$= + - A \uparrow B3/C \uparrow D2$

20. Convert the following prefix to infix notation:

$$+ - AC * A/CB$$

$= (A - C) + * A/CB$
$= (A - C) + A * \frac{C}{B}$

21. Convert the following infix to postfix notation:

$$A - \frac{B}{B} + \frac{B^2}{B^2} + A$$

$= ((A - (\frac{B}{B})) + (\frac{B^2}{B^2})) + A$

$= ((A - (BB/)) + (\frac{B^2}{B^2})) + A$

$= ((ABB/-) + (\frac{B^2}{B^2})) + A$

$= ((ABB/-) + (\frac{B2\uparrow}{B2\uparrow})) + A$

$= ((ABB/-) + (B2\uparrow B2\uparrow/)) + A$
$= (ABB/-B2\uparrow B2\uparrow/+) + A$
$= ABB/-B2\uparrow B2\uparrow/+A+$

Test 2

22. Convert the following infix notation to post fix notation:
$$(A - B) * (B - \frac{C}{D})$$

$= (A - B) * (B - (\frac{C}{D}))$
$= (A - B) * (B - (CD/))$
$= (A - B) * (BCD/-)$
$= (AB -) * (BCD/-)$
$= AB - BCD/- *$

23. Convert the following infix to prefix notation:
$$\frac{A}{A - C} + B * (C - D)$$

$= (\frac{A}{(A - C)}) + (B * (C - D))$
$= (\frac{A}{(-AC)}) + (B * (C - D))$
$= (/A - AC) + (B * (C - D))$
$= (/A - AC) + (B * (-CD))$
$= (/A - AC) + (* B - CD)$
$= +/A - AC * B - CD$

24. Convert the following infix to postfix notation:
$$A - B + \frac{C}{D}$$

$= (A - B) + (\frac{C}{D})$
$= (A - B) + (CD/)$
$= (AB-) + (CD/)$
$= AB - CD/+$

25. Convert the following infix into prefix notation:
$$A * B * \frac{C}{D} * A$$

$= ((A * B) * (\frac{C}{D})) * A$
$= ((A * B) * (/CD)) * A$
$= ((* AB) * (/CD)) * A$
$= (** AB/CD) * A$
$= *** AB/CDA$

ACSL
Pre/Post/In - fix Notation

Test 2

26. Convert the following infix into postfix notation

$$(A - B) + \left(\frac{A}{B}\right)^2$$

$= (A - B) + (AB/)^2$
$= (A - B) + (AB/2 \uparrow)$
$= (AB -) + (AB/2 \uparrow)$
$= AB - AB/2 \uparrow +$

27. Convert the following infix to prefix notation:

$$(A - B)^2 + (B * C)^3$$

$= [(-AB)^2 + (*BC)^3]$
$= [(\uparrow -AB2) + (\uparrow * BC3)]$
$= +\uparrow -AB2 \uparrow * BC3$

28. Convert the following infix to prefix notation:

$$A - \left[\frac{B+C}{D}\right]^2 + (A * C)$$

$= (A - [\frac{+BC}{D}]^2) + (*AC)$
$= (A - [/+BCD]^2) + (*AC)$
$= (-A \uparrow /+BCD2) + (*AC)$
$= +-A \uparrow /+BCD2 * AC$

29. Convert the following infix to prefix notation:

$$A * C^3 + D^4 + C^2 * D$$

$= ((A * C^3) + D^4) + (C^2 * D)$
$= ((A * \uparrow C3) + D^4) + (C^2 * D)$
$= ((*A \uparrow C3) + D^4) + (C^2 * D)$
$= ((*A \uparrow C3) + (\uparrow D4)) + (C^2 * D)$
$= (+ * A \uparrow C3 \uparrow D4) + (C^2 * D)$
$= (+ * A \uparrow C3 \uparrow D4) + ((\uparrow C2) * D)$
$= (+ * A \uparrow C3 \uparrow D4) + (*\uparrow C2D)$
$= + + * A \uparrow C3 \uparrow D4 *\uparrow C2D$

Test 2

30. Convert the following infix to postfix notation:
$$\frac{A+B}{A-C} + C - D$$

$= [(\frac{(A+B)}{(A-C)}) + C] - D$

$= [(\frac{(AB+)}{(AC-)}) + C] - D$

$= [(AB + AC -/) + C] - D$

$= [AB + AC -/C +] - D$

$= AB + AC -/C + D -$

31. Convert the following infix to prefix notation:
$$[\frac{A+B}{A+C}]^E * [\frac{C*D}{C*B}]^F$$

$= ([\frac{(A+B)}{(A+C)}]^E) * ([\frac{(C*D)}{(C*B)}]^F)$

$= ([\frac{(+AB)}{(+AC)}]^E) * ([\frac{(C*D)}{(C*B)}]^F)$

$= ([/+AB+AC]^E) * ([\frac{(C*D)}{(C*B)}]^F)$

$= (\uparrow/+AB+ACE) * ([\frac{(C*D)}{(C*B)}]^F)$

$= (\uparrow/+AB+ACE) * ([\frac{(*CD)}{(*CB)}]^F)$

$= (\uparrow/+AB+ACE) * ([/*CD*CB]^F)$

$= (\uparrow/+AB+ACE) * (\uparrow/*CD*CBF)$

$= *\uparrow/+AB+ACE\uparrow/*CD*CBF$

32. Convert the following postfix to infix notation and find the final answer:
$$AB*G \uparrow BC/F \uparrow +CD/E \uparrow +$$
where $A = C = 88; B = D = 90; E = F = G = 0$

$= (A*B)^G BC/F \uparrow +CD/E \uparrow +$

$= (A*B)^G + (\frac{B}{C})^F CD/E \uparrow +$

$= (A*B)^G + (\frac{B}{C})^F + (\frac{C}{D})^E$

Because the powers E, F and G are '0', therefore the final answer will be 3.

Test 2

33. Convert the following infix to prefix notations:
$$A + \frac{A}{B} + \frac{B}{A} * A$$

$= ((A + (\frac{A}{B})) + ((\frac{B}{A}) * A))$

$= ((A + (/AB)) + ((/BA) * A))$

$= ((A + (/AB)) + (*/BAA))$

$= ((+A/AB) + (*/BAA))$

$= + + A/AB */BAA$

34. Convert the following infix to postfix notation:
$$\frac{A-B}{B^2} + \frac{C-D}{C^3}$$

$= (\frac{(A-B)}{B^2}) + (\frac{(C-D)}{C^3})$

$= (\frac{(AB-)}{B2\uparrow}) + (\frac{(C-D)}{C^3})$

$= (AB - B2 \uparrow /) + (\frac{(C-D)}{C^3})$

$= (AB - B2 \uparrow /) + (\frac{(CD-)}{C3 \uparrow})$

$= (AB - B2 \uparrow /) + (CD - C3 \uparrow /)$

$= AB - B2 \uparrow / CD - CC3 \uparrow / +$

35. Convert the following postfix to infix notation and find the final answer:
$$AB \uparrow 2 - \frac{CD}{+}, where\ A = B = 2; C = D = -2$$

$= A - B^2 + \frac{C}{D}$

$= 2 - 2^2 + \frac{(-2)}{(-2)} = -1$

36. Convert the following infix to prefix notation:
$$\frac{A-B}{B-A} + (A^B * B^A)$$

$= (\frac{(A-B)}{(B-A)}) + (A^B * B^A)$

$= (\frac{(-AB)}{(-BA)}) + (A^B * B^A)$

$= (/-AB - BA) + ((\uparrow AB) * (\uparrow BA))$

$= (/-AB - BA) + (*\uparrow AB \uparrow BA)$

$= +/-AB - BA *\uparrow AB \uparrow BA$

37. Convert the following infix to postfix notation:
$$\frac{C}{D} + A^2 + B^3$$

$= ((\frac{C}{D}) + (A^2)) + (B^3)$

$= ((CD/) + (A2\uparrow)) + (B3\uparrow)$
$= (CD/A2\uparrow +) + (B3\uparrow)$
$= CD/A2\uparrow +B3\uparrow +$

38. Convert the following infix to prefix notation:
$$A^A * \frac{A^A}{B^B}$$

$= A^A * (\frac{A^A}{B^B})$

$= A^A * (\frac{\uparrow AA}{\uparrow BB})$

$= A^A * (/\uparrow AA \uparrow BB)$
$= \uparrow AA * (/\uparrow AA \uparrow BB)$
$= *\uparrow AA/\uparrow AA \uparrow BB$

39. Convert the following infix to postfix notation:
$$A * B + B + A - \frac{C^C}{A - C}$$

$= (((A*B) + B) + A) - (\frac{(C^C)}{(A-C)})$

$= (((AB*) + B) + A) - (\frac{CC\uparrow}{(AC-)})$

$= ((AB*B+) + A) - (\frac{CC\uparrow}{(AC-)})$

$= (AB*B+A+) - (CC\uparrow AC-/)$
$= AB*B+A+ CC\uparrow AC-/-$

40. Convert the following infix to postfix notation:
$$[\frac{A+B}{A}]^2 * [\frac{C-D}{C}]^3$$

$= [\frac{(A+B)}{A}]^2 * [\frac{(C-D)}{C}]^3$

$= [\frac{AB+}{A}]^2 * [\frac{(C-D)}{C}]^3$

$= [AB+A/]^2 * [\frac{(C-D)}{C}]^3$

$= [AB+A/2\uparrow] * [\frac{(CD-)}{C}]^3$

$= [AB+A/2\uparrow] * [CD-C/3\uparrow]$
$= AB+A/2\uparrow CD-C/3\uparrow *$

ACSL — Pre/Post/In - fix Notation

Test 2

41. Convert the following infix to prefix notation:

$$\frac{A-B}{A^2-B^2} + C^3 - \frac{D^2}{A^2}$$

$= ((\frac{(A-B)}{(A^2-B^2)}) + C^3) - (\frac{D^2}{A^2})$

$= ((\frac{(-AB)}{((\uparrow A2)-(\uparrow B2))}) + \uparrow C3) - (\frac{D^2}{A^2})$

$= ((/-AB-\uparrow A2 \uparrow B2) + (\uparrow C3)) - (\frac{D^2}{A^2})$

$= (+/-AB-\uparrow A2 \uparrow B2 \uparrow C3) - (\frac{D^2}{A^2})$

$= (+/-AB-\uparrow A2 \uparrow B2 \uparrow C3) - (\frac{\uparrow D2}{\uparrow A2})$

$= (+/-AB-\uparrow A2 \uparrow B2 \uparrow C3) - (/\uparrow D2 \uparrow A2)$

$= -+/-AB-\uparrow A2 \uparrow B2 \uparrow C3/\uparrow D2 \uparrow A2$

42. Convert the following infix to postfix notation:

$$(A - B^3 + \frac{C^4}{A^3} + (B*C))$$

$= ((A-(B^3)) + (\frac{C^4}{A^3}) + (B*C)$

$= ((A-(B3\uparrow)) + (\frac{C4\uparrow}{A3\uparrow}) + (B*C)$

$= (AB3\uparrow-) + (C4\uparrow A3\uparrow/) + (BC*)$

$= (AB3\uparrow-C4\uparrow A3\uparrow/+) + (BC*)$

$= AB3\uparrow-C4\uparrow A3\uparrow/+BC*+$

43. Convert the following infix to prefix notations:

$$A^2 - [\frac{B+C}{D^2}]^2 + (A*C)^2$$

$= (\uparrow A2 - [\frac{+BC}{\uparrow D2}]^2) + (A*C)^2$

$= (\uparrow A2 - [/+BC \uparrow D2]^2) + (A*C)^2$

$= (-\uparrow A2 \uparrow/+BC \uparrow D22) + (*AC)^2$

$= (-\uparrow A2 \uparrow/+BC \uparrow D22) + (\uparrow* AC2)$

$= +-\uparrow A2 \uparrow/+BC \uparrow D22 \uparrow* AC2$

ACSL Pre/Post/In-fix Notation

Test 2

44. Convert the following infix to postfix notation:
$$X^2 + \frac{Y^X}{X^3} - \frac{Y-X}{X*Y}$$

$= X^2 + (\frac{Y^X}{X^3}) - (\frac{Y-X}{X*Y})$

$= X2\uparrow + (\frac{YX\uparrow}{X3\uparrow}) - (\frac{YX-}{XY*})$

$= X2\uparrow +(Y\uparrow XX\uparrow 3/) - (YX - XY*/)$

$= (X2\uparrow Y\uparrow XX\uparrow 3/+) - (YX - XY*/)$

$= X\uparrow 2Y\uparrow XX\uparrow 3/+YX - XY*/-$

45. Convert the following postfix to infix notation and evaluate the final answer:
$$2 3/ 4 + 4 5/ -4 2 \uparrow -$$

$= \frac{2}{3} + 4 - \frac{4}{5} - 4^2 = -\frac{182}{15}$

46. Evaluate "S" in prefix form:
$$S = \frac{P^2}{Q^3} + \frac{(P-Q)}{P^R}$$

$S = \frac{P^2}{Q^3} + (\frac{(-PQ)}{P^R})$

$S = \frac{\uparrow P2}{\uparrow Q3} + (\frac{(-PQ)}{\uparrow PR})$

$S = (/\uparrow P2 \uparrow Q3) + (/-PQ \uparrow PR)$

$S = (/\uparrow P2 \uparrow Q3) + (/-PQ \uparrow PR)$

$S = +/\uparrow P2 \uparrow Q3/-PQ \uparrow PR$

47. Convert the following infix to postfix notation:
$$O^T - \frac{P^S}{P^P} + (O-P), where\ T = 2\ and\ S = 3$$

According to the question,

$= O^2 - \frac{P^3}{P^P} + (O-P)$

$= O^2 - (\frac{P^3}{P^P}) + (O-P)$

$= (O2\uparrow) - (\frac{P3\uparrow}{PP\uparrow}) + (OP-)$

$= (O2\uparrow P3\uparrow PP\uparrow /-) + (OP-)$

$= O2\uparrow P3\uparrow PP\uparrow /-OP-+$

Test 2

48. Convert the following prefix to infix notation:
$$-+/25/43-43$$

$$\frac{2}{5}+\frac{4}{3}-(4-3)=\frac{11}{15}$$

49. Convert the following infix to prefix notation:
$$\frac{(\frac{A-C}{A+C})}{\frac{A}{C}}$$

$$=\frac{(\frac{A-C}{A+C})}{(\frac{A}{C})}$$

$$=\frac{(\frac{-AC}{+AC})}{(\frac{A}{C})}$$

$$=\frac{(/-AC+AC)}{(/AC)}$$

$$=//-AC+AC/AC$$

50. Evaluate the expression for "R" in postfix form:
$$R=\frac{(\frac{P-Q^2}{P^2+Q})}{(P-\frac{Q}{2})}$$

$$R=\frac{(\frac{P-(Q2\uparrow)}{(P\uparrow 2)+Q})}{(P-\frac{Q}{2})}$$

$$R=\frac{(\frac{PQ2\uparrow -}{P2\uparrow Q+})}{(P-\frac{Q}{2})}$$

$$R=\frac{(PQ2\uparrow -P2\uparrow Q+/)}{(P-\frac{Q}{2})}$$

$$R=\frac{(PQ2\uparrow -P2\uparrow Q+/)}{(P-(Q2/))}$$

$$R=\frac{(PQ2\uparrow -P2\uparrow Q+/)}{(P-(Q2/))}$$

$$R=\frac{(PQ2\uparrow -P2\uparrow Q+/)}{(PQ2/-)}$$

$$R=PQ2\uparrow -P2\uparrow Q+/PQ2/-/$$

ACSL
Bit String Flicking

Test 2

1. (RSHIFT-1 (LCIRC-2 (RCIRC-1 01110)))
   = (RSHIFT-1 (LCIRC-2 00111))
   = (RSHIFT-1 11100)
   = 01110

2. (LSHIFT-2 (LSHIFT-2 (RCIRC-1 1111011)))
   = (LSHIFT-2 (LSHIFT-2 1111101))
   = (LSHIFT-2 1110100)
   = 1010000

3. (LCIRC-1 (RCIRC-1 11110 OR LCIRC-2 11001))
   (LCIRC-1 (01111 OR 00111))
   (LCIRC-1 01111)
   11110

4. (RCIRC-3 (LCIRC-1 111001 OR LSHIFT-2 100111))
   = (RCIRC-3 (110011 OR 011100))
   = (RCIRC-3 111111)
   = 111111

5. (RCIRC-1 111001001 OR RSHIFT-2 100100111)
   = (111100100 OR 001001001)
   = 111101101

6. (LSHIFT-2 (LSHIFT-2 (RCIRC-1 11011))) OR LSHIFT-1 10001
   = (LSHIFT-2 (LSHIFT-2 11101)) OR 00010
   = (LSHIFT-2 10100) OR 00010
   = 10000 OR 00010
   = 10010

7. (LCIRC-3 (RCIRC-2 101011)) AND RSHIFT-1 100010
   = (LCIRC-3 111010) AND 010001
   = 010111 AND 010001
   = 010001

8. (RSHIFT-3 (LCIRC-2 (RCIRC-3 10111011)))
   = (RSHIFT-3 (LCIRC-2 01110111))
   = (RSHIFT-3 (11011101))
   = 00011011

9. (LSHIFT-3 (LSHIFT-2 (RCIRC-4 000001111))) OR (LSHIFT-3 111110000)
   = (LSHIFT-3 (LSHIFT-2 111100000)) OR 110000000
   = (LSHIFT-3 110000000) OR 110000000
   = 000000000 OR 110000000
   = 000000000 OR 110000000
   = 110000000

10. (LCIRC-1 11001001 OR LSHIFT-2 10010011)
    = 10010011 OR 01001100
    = 11011111

11. (LCIRC-1 (LCIRC-2 1011)) AND RSHIFT-1 1010
    = (LCIRC-1 0111) AND 0101
    = 1110 AND 0101
    = 0100

12. (LCIRC-3 (LCIRC-2 101010)) AND (LSHIFT-1 (RSHIFT-1 110010))
    = (LCIRC-3 101010) AND (LSHIFT-1 011001)
    = 010101 AND 110010
    = 010000

13. (RCIRC-3 101111)) XOR RSHIFT-1 111010
    = 111101 XOR 011101
    = 100000

14. (LSHIFT-2 (RSHIFT-2 (LCIRC-3 010001111))) XOR (LSHIFT-3 111110010)
    = (LSHIFT-2 (RSHIFT-2 001111010)) XOR 110010000
    = (LSHIFT-2 000011110) XOR 110010000
    = 001111000 XOR 110010000
    = 111101000

15. (LSHIFT-3 (RCIRC-2 000001111)) XOR (LSHIFT-2 111110000)
    = (LSHIFT-3 110000011) XOR 111000000
    = 000011000 XOR 111000000
    = 111011000

16. NOT (LSHIFT-2 (LCIRC-2 000001111))
    = NOT (LSHIFT-2 000111100)
    = NOT 011110000
    = 100001111

17. 1000111 XOR (LSHIFT-4 (RCIRC-2 0101011))
    = 1000111 XOR (LSHIFT-4 1101010)
    = 1000111 XOR 0100000
    = 1100111

18. NOT (RSHIFT-3 (RCIRC-2 110001111))
    = NOT (RSHIFT-3 111100011)
    = NOT 000111100
    =111000011

19. (RCIRC-2 101011) OR (RSHIFT-1 111010)
    = 111010 OR 011101
    = 111111

20. NOT (LSHIFT-2 (RSHIFT-3 (RCIRC-3 001111)))
    = NOT (LSHIFT-2 (RSHIFT-3 111001))
    = NOT (LSHIFT-2 000111)
    = NOT 011100
    = 100011

21. ((LCIRC-3 (10110 OR 11010)) AND (LSHIFT-1 10111))
    = (LCIRC-3 11110) AND (01110)
    = (10111) AND (01110)
    = 00110

22. (RCIRC-2 1001010) AND (RSHIFT-1 1010011)
    = (1010010) AND (0101001)
    = 0000000

23. ((RSHIFT-2 (1010010 AND 1001010)) OR (LSHIFT-1 1011001))
    = ((RSHIFT-2 (1010010 AND 1001010)) OR 0110010)
    = ((RSHIFT-2 1000010) OR 0110010)
    = (0010000) OR 0110010)
    = 0110010

24. NOT ((00011 XOR 10101) AND 11100)
    = NOT ((10110) AND 11100)
    = NOT (10100)
    = 01011

ACSL
Bit String Flicking

Test 2

25. NOT ((0000011 XOR 1010001) OR 1001100)
    = NOT ((1010010) OR 1001100))
    = NOT ((1011110))
    = NOT (1011110)
    = 0100001

26. LSHIFT-1 (NOT ((00011 XOR 10001) OR 10100))
    = LSHIFT-1 (NOT ((10010) OR 10100))
    = LSHIFT-1 (NOT (10110))
    = LSHIFT-1 01001
    = 10010

27. (RSHIFT-2 (00000 XOR 10100)) AND (NOT 00011)
    = (RSHIFT-2 10100) AND (11100)
    = (00101) AND (11100)
    = 00100

28. (RSHIFT-3 (1000010 XOR 1101000)) AND (RSHIFT-3 1011001)
    = (RSHIFT-3 (0101010)) AND (0001011)
    = (0000101) AND (0001011)
    = 0000001

29. (NOT (100011 OR 100111)) OR (100010 AND (100011))
    = (NOT (100111)) OR 100010
    = 011000 OR 100010
    = 111010

30. (10010 OR 10011) AND (00000 AND (10000))
    = 10011 AND 00000
    = 00000

31. (LSHIFT-3 (RSHIFT-2 (LCIRC-1 11011))) OR LSHIFT-4 10001
    = (LSHIFT-3 (RSHIFT-2 10111)) OR 10000
    = (LSHIFT-3 00101) OR 10000
    = 01000 OR 10000
    = 11000

32. (RCIRC-2 (LCIRC-3 101001)) AND RSHIFT-2 110010
    = (RCIRC-2 001101) AND RSHIFT-2 110010
    = 010011 AND 001101
    = 000001

33. (RSHIFT-2 (RCIRC-1 (LCIRC-2 100010))) XOR 100001
    = (RSHIFT-2 (RCIRC-1 001010)) XOR 100001
    = (RSHIFT-2 000101) XOR 100001
    = 000001 XOR 100001
    = 100000

34. (LSHIFT-2 (LSHIFT-2 (RCIRC-2 001111))) OR (LSHIFT-2 (RCIRC-1 111000))
    = (LSHIFT-2 (LSHIFT-2 110011)) OR (LSHIFT-2 011100)
    = (LSHIFT-2 001100) OR (LSHIFT-2 011100)
    = (110000) OR (110000)
    = 110000

35. (LCIRC-1 110010 OR LSHIFT-2 100101) AND (NOT 111000)
    = (100101 OR 010100) AND (000111)
    = 110101 AND 000111
    = 000101

36. (LCIRC-2 (LCIRC-1 10011)) AND (RSHIFT-2 (LCIRC-2 10100))
    = (LCIRC-2 00111) AND (RSHIFT-2 10010)
    = 11100 AND 00100
    = 00100

37. (LCIRC-2 (LCIRC-1 100010)) AND (RSHIFT-1 (RSHIFT-1 100000))
    = (LCIRC-2 000101) AND (RSHIFT-1 010000)
    = 010100 AND 001000
    = 000000

38. (RCIRC-3 101111)) XOR (RSHIFT-1 (LCIRC-2 111010))
    = (111101)) XOR (RSHIFT-1 101011)
    = (111101) XOR (010101)
    = 101000

39. NOT ((((LSHIFT-3 (RSHIFT-2 (LCIRC-2 010001111))) OR (LSHIFT-2 111110010))
    = NOT (((LSHIFT-3 (RSHIFT-2 000111101)) OR 111001000)
    = NOT ((LSHIFT-3 000001111 OR 111001000)
    = NOT ((001111000) OR 111001000)
    = NOT 111111000
    = 000000111

40. (LSHIFT-2 (RCIRC-2 001001111)) OR (RSHIFT-2 110110000)
    = (LSHIFT-2 (110010011)) OR (001101100)
    = (001001100) OR (001101100)
    = 001101100

Test 2

41. (NOT (RSHIFT-3 (LCIRC-2 000001111))) OR 100000001
    = (NOT (RSHIFT-3 000111100)) OR 100000001
    = (NOT (000000111)) OR 100000001
    = 111111000 OR 100000001
    = 111111001

42. 100011 XOR (LSHIFT-4 (RCIRC-2 010011))
    = 100011 XOR (LSHIFT-4 110100)
    = 100011 XOR 000000
    = 100011

43. (LCIRC-2 (LCIRC-2 1000011)) AND (RSHIFT-2 1000010)
    = (LCIRC-2 (0001110)) AND (0010000)
    = (0111000) AND (0010000)
    = 0010000

44. (LCIRC-3 (LCIRC-3 101010)) XOR (LSHIFT-2 (RSHIFT-1 110010))
    = (LCIRC-3 (010101)) XOR (LSHIFT-2 (011001))
    = (101010) XOR (100100)
    = 001110

45. ((RCIRC-3 100000 XOR RSHIFT-1 111010) OR (NOT (000001 AND 111110))
    = (000100 XOR 011101) OR (NOT (000000))
    = (011001) OR (NOT (000000))
    = (011001) OR (111111)
    = 111111

46. (LSHIFT-2 (RSHIFT-4 (LCIRC-3 0101111))) XOR (LSHIFT-2 1111110)
    = (LSHIFT-2 (RSHIFT-4 1111010)) XOR (1111000)
    = (LSHIFT-2 (0000111)) XOR (1111000)
    = (0011100) XOR (1111000)
    =1100100

47. (RSHIFT-4 (LCIRC-2 000001111)) OR (RSHIFT-2 111110000)
    = (RSHIFT-4 (000111100)) OR (001111100)
    = (000000011) OR (001111100)
    = 001111111

48. (NOT (LSHIFT-2 (LCIRC-2 11110000))) OR (LSHIFT-1 10101010)
    = (NOT (LSHIFT-2 (11000011))) OR (01010100)
    = (NOT (LSHIFT-2 00001100)) OR (01010100)
    = (NOT 00110000) OR (01010100)
    = 11001111 OR 01010100
    = 11011111

49. 1000101 OR (LSHIFT-4 (RCIRC-2 (LSHIFT-2 0101001))
    = 1000101 OR (LSHIFT-4 (RCIRC-2 0100100))
    = 1000101 OR (LSHIFT-4 0001001)
    = 1000101 OR 0010000
    = 1010101

50. NOT (LSHIFT-3 (RCIRC-2 (LCIRC-4 110001111))
    = NOT (LSHIFT-3 (RCIRC-2 011111100))
    = NOT (LSHIFT-3 000111111)
    = NOT (111111000)
    = 000000111

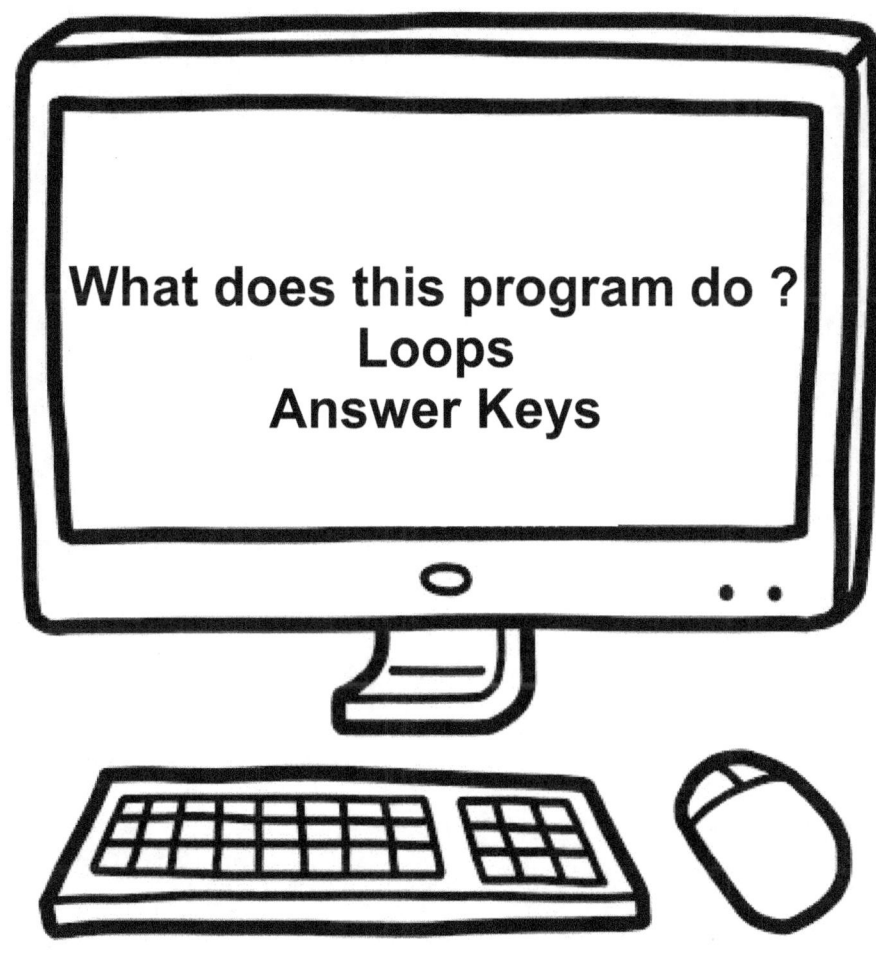

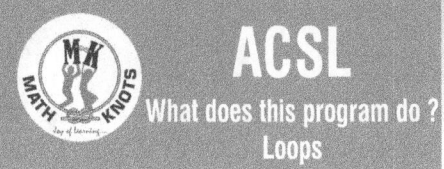

Test 2

1. What can the program do?
   ```
   for i = 1 to 5
      for j = 2 to 5
         k = i/j
         if k>2
            Output k
         end
      end
   end
   ```

   Output
   2.5

2. What can the program do?
   ```
   k = 0
   for i = 1 to 6
      k = k+i
      if k>5
         PRINT k
      end
   end
   ```

   Output
   6

   10

   15

   21

3. What will the output of the program?
   ```
   k = 0
   for i = 1 to 5
      k = k+i
      if k<5
         PRINT small
      else
         Output big
      end
   end
   ```

   Output
   small
   small
   big
   big
   big

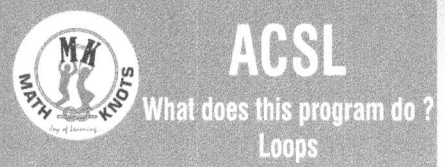

4. What is the output of the program?
```
a = 2
for i = 2:2:10
    a = a+i/2
    if a<(i+2)
        Output "*"
    elseif a>(i+2)
        Output "$"
    else
        Output "%"
    end

end
```

Output
```
*
*
%
$
$
```

5. What is the output of the program?
```
int rows, i, j, space;
rows=4
for (i=1; i<=rows;i++)
    for (j=1; j<=(2*i-1);j++)
        Output "$"
    Output "\n"
```

Output
```
$
$$
$$$
$$$$
```

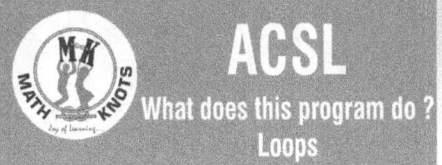

6. What is the output of the program?
```
a = 2
for i = 0 to 8
    i = i+2
    a = a+i/2
    if a<(i/2)
        Output i
    elseif a>(i/2)
        Output i+1
    else
        Output 0
    end
end
```

Output
3
5
7
9

7. What is the output of the program?
```
a = 1
for i = 2 to 4
    j = 1
    a = a*i
    if a>(2*j)
        a=i
        Output i
    else
        Output 0
    end
end
```

Output
0
3
4

8. What is the output of the program?
   ```
   a = 2
   for i = 0 to 8
       i= i+2
      %for j = 2 to 3
      j=1
      a = a*$\frac{i}{2}$
      if a>(2*j)
         a=i
         Output "*"
      else
         Output "-"
      end
   end
   ```

   Output
   ```
   -
   *
   *
   *
   ```

9. What is the output of the program?
   ```
   a = 2
   for i = 0 to 8
       i=i+2
      j=i
      a = a*$\frac{i}{2}$
      if a>(2+j)
         PRINT j
      else
         PRINT i
      end
   end
   ```

   Output
   ```
   2
   4
   6
   8
   ```

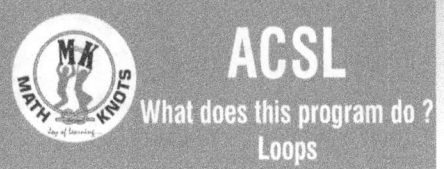

10. What is the output of the program?
```
a = 2
for z = 0 to 8
    z=z+2
    j=z
    a = a*z/2
    if a>(2+j)
       t = a
         PRINT t
    else
         PRINT "null"
    end

end
```

Output
null
null
12
48

11. What is the output of the program?
```
a = 2
for z = 0 to 4
     z = z+2
    a = a*z/2
    if a>(1+z)
       t = a
         Output t
    else
         Output "null"
    end

end
```

Output
null
null
null
15
45

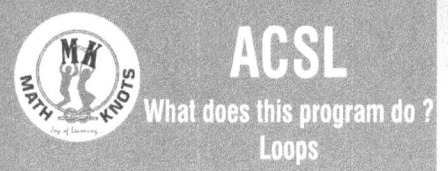

12. What is the output of the program?
    ```
    o = 2
    for z = 2 to 6
        o = o*z/2
        if o>(1+z)
           t = o
           if t>20
              Output t
           end
        else
           Output "null"
        end
    end
    ```

    Output
    Null
    Null
    45

13. What is the output of the program?
    ```
    b = 1 ;
    for x = 1:2:5
        c = b/2
        a = x*c*2
        if a>18
           Output a
        else
           c = b/2
           Output c
        end
     end
    ```

    Output
    0.5000
    0.5000
    0.5000

14. What is the output of the program?
    ```
    for x = 2 to 6
        y=x+1
        if x < 5
        Output y
        end
    end
    ```
    Output
    3
    4
    5

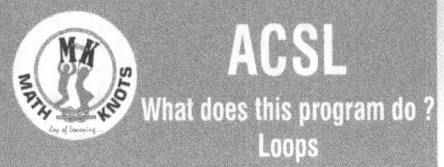

Test 2

15. What is the output of the program?
```
a = 't'
for x = 2 to 10
   y = a
   if x>6
      Output "s"
   else
      Output a
   end

end
```
Output
t
t
t
t
t
s
s
s
s

16. What is the output of the program?
```
for x = 2 to 4
   y = [ 1 0 ; 0 1]
   z = y*y
end
```
Output
1   0
0   1

17. What is the output of the program?
```
c = 1
for x = 1 to 6
   b = x/2
   a = x*b*2
   if a>5
      Output a
   else
      c = x/2
      Output c
   end
 end
```
Output
0.5000
1
9
16
25
36

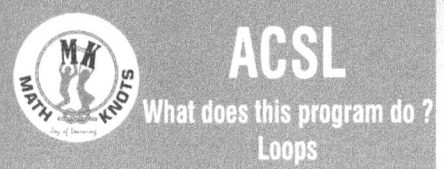

Test 2

18. What is the output of the program?
    for x = 2 to 4
       y = [1 0 ; 0 1]
       z = y+y
    end

    Output
    2 0
    0 2

19. What is the output?
    int i, x;
    int m =4
    for (i=m; i>=m; i - -)
    for (x=1; x<=1; j++)
    Output "|"
    Output "\n"

    Output
    ||||
    |||
    ||
    |

20. What is the output of the program?
    c = 1
    for x = 1:2:6
       b = x
       a = x*$\frac{b}{2}$
       if a>5
          Output a
       else
          c=$\frac{x}{2}$
          Output c
       end
    end

    output
     0.5000
     1.5000
    12 5000

21. What is the output of the program?
    ```
    c = 1
    for x = 1:2:5
        b = c/2
        a = x*c*2
        if a>5
            Output a
        else
            c = b/2
            Output c
        end
    end
    ```

    Output
    0.2500
    0.0625
    0.0156

22. What is the result after the entire loop?
    ```
    for x = 1:2:5
        for y = 1:3
            z = x*y
            z = z+1
        output z
        end
    end
    ```

    Output
    16

23. What is the value of a and b after the looping?
    ```
    for x = 1:2:5
        for y = 1:3
            if x<y || x == y
                a = x² + y²
            else
                b = x/y
            end
        end
    end
    ```

    Output
    a = 18
    b = 1.6667

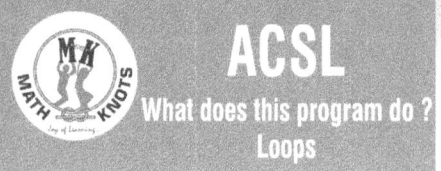

24. What is the value of a, b and c the program?
    for x = 1:2:5
      for y = 1:3
        if x<y
          a = x^2
        elseif x>y
          b = y^2
        else
          c = $\frac{x}{y}$
        end
      end
    end

Output
a = 1
b = 9
c = 1

25. What is the output of the program?
    s = 0
    for x = 1:4
      a = x
      b = x^a
      s = s+b
    end

Output
288

26. What is the output of every loop?
    s = 0
    for x = 1:4
    for x = 1:2:8
      if x>4
        x = x^2
      elseif x<4
        x = 2*x
      else
        x = $\frac{x}{2}$
      end
    end

Output
49

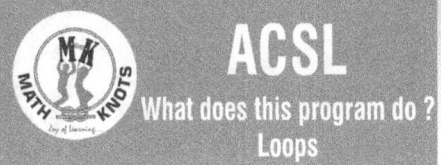

30. What is the output if rows=3?
    ```
    int i, j, space;
    int rows = 3;
    for (i=1; i<=rows;i++)
     for (j=1; j<=(2*i-1);j++)
    Output "*"
    Output "\n"
    ```

    Output

    ```
    *
    **
    ***
    ```

31. What is the output of the loop?
    ```
    for x = 2:2:8
      if x>4
        x = x²
      elseif x<4
        x = 2*x
      else
        x = x/2
      end
    end
    ```

    Output
    4
    2
    36
    64

32. What is the output of the program?
    ```
    s = 0
    for x = 2:2:8
      for y = 1:3
        s = s+x
      end
    end
    ```

    Output
    s = 60

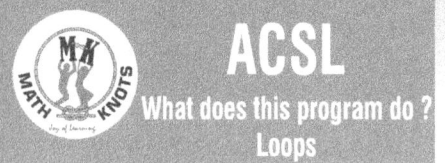

Test 2

33. What is the value of u in the program?
    ```
    s = 2
    for x = 1:5
      s = s+x
      t = s*2
      u = t/s ;
    end
    ```

    Output
    u = 2

34. What is the output of the program?
    ```
    s = 2
    a = 1
    b =
    for x = 1:5
      c = a*b
      c = c+2
    end
    ```

    Output
    c = 3

35. What is the output?
    ```
    int m, i, j;
    m=2
    for (i=m; i>=m; i -- )
    for (j=1; j<=1; j++)
    Output "*"
    Output "\n"
    ```

    Output
    ```
    **
    *
    ```

36. What is the output of the program?
    ```
    sum = 0;
    for(c = 1; c <=5; ++c)
    sum += c ;
    Output sum
    ```

    Output
    15

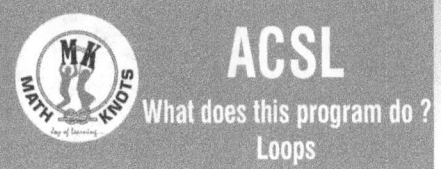

Test 2

37. What is the output of the program?
```
for x = 1:8
  if x<2
     Output "$\n"
  elseif x>2 && x<4
     Output "**\n"
  elseif x>4 && x<6
     Output "*$*\n"
  else
     Output "$$$\n"
  end
end
```
Output
$
$$$
**
$$$
$
$$$
$$$
$$$

38. What is the output of the program?
```
sum = 0
for(i = 1; i <= 10; i++)
Output "%d * %d = %d \n", 5, i, 5*i)
```
Output
5*1=5
5*2=10
5*3=15
5*4=20
5*5=25
5*6=30
5*7=35
5*8=40
5*9=45
5*10=50

39. What is the output of the program?
```
sum = 0
n = 10
for (i = 1; i <= 5; i++)
Output "%d / %d = %d \n", n, i, n/I"
```
Output
5/1 = 5
5/2 = 2.5
5/3 = 1.4
5/4 = 1.25
5/5 = 1

40. What is the output of the program?
    long long n
    int c = 0
    n = 5124
    while (n !=0)
    n/=10;
    ++c;
    Output c

    Output
    4

41. What is the output of the program?
    int number = 40
    if(number %2 == 0)
    Output "%d is even"
    else
    Output "%d is odd"

    Output
    40 is even

42. What is the output of the program rows = 5?
    int rows, i, j, space;
    rows=3
    for (i=1; i<=rows;i++)
    for (j=1; j<=(2*i-1);j++)
    Output "*"
    Output "\n"

    Output

    *
    **
    ***
    ****
    *****

43. What is the value of q and r in the program?
    int n = 20, i = 3
    int quotient, remainder
    $q = \frac{n}{i}$
    r = n%i
    Output
    Output r

    Output
    q = 6
    r = 2

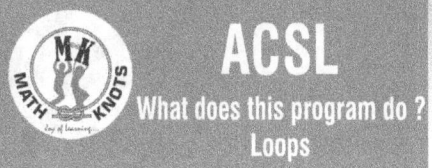

ACSL
What does this program do ?
Loops

Test 2

44. What is the output of the program?
    sum =
    n = 5
    for(i = 1; i <= n; i++)
    sum = sum+i
    Output sum

    Output
    17

45. What is the output of the program after the loop is executed?
    sum = 0
    n = 10
    for(i = 1; i <= 5; i++)
    sum = $(sum * n + sum)^0$

    Output
    1

46. What is the output of the program?
    s = 2
    a = 1
    b = 1
    for x = 1:5
      if x<3
        s=a^2+b^2
      elseif x>3
        s=$\frac{a}{b}$
      else
        s =0
    end
    end

    Output
    2
    2
    0
    1
    1

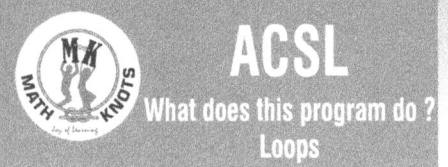

47. What is the output of the program?
    ```
    s = 2
    a = 1
    b = 1
    for x = 1:5
      if x<3
          s=a²+b/2
      elseif x>3
          Output "termination"
          break
      else
          s =0
      end
    end
    ```

    Output
    1.5
    1.5
    0
    termination

48. What is the output of the program?
    ```
    s = 5
    a = 1.5
    b = 2
    for x = 1:5
      if x<3
          s=a/2 + b/2
      elseif x>3
          Output "termination"
          break
      else
          Output "-\n"
      end
    end
    ```

    Output
    1.7500
    1.7500
    -
    termination

ACSL
What does this program do?
Loops

Test 2

49. What is the output of the program?
    ```
    for x = 1:5
      if x<2
        Output "*\n"
      elseif x>2 && x<4
        Output "**\n"
      elseif x>4
        Output "***\n"
      else
        Output "$$$"

    end
    end
    ```

    Output
    ```
    *
    $$$**
    $$$***
    ```

50. What is the output of the program if rows =4?
    ```
    int rows, i, j, space;
    rows=4
    for (i=1; i<=rows;i++)
    for (space = i; space<rows; space++)
    Output " "
    for (j=1; j<=(2*i-1);j++)
    Output "*"
    Output "\n"
    ```

    Output
    ```
       *
      **
     ***
    ****
    ```

www.ingramcontent.com/pod-product-compliance
Lightning Source LLC
Chambersburg PA
CBHW081151290426
44108CB00018B/2506